Haunted Plantations
of Virginia

Beth Brown

Schiffer Publishing Ltd

4880 Lower Valley Road, Atglen Pennsylvania 19310

Other books by author:
Haunted Battlefields, **978-0-7643-3057-5, $14.99**

Unless otherwise noted, photographs are courtesy of the author.

Published by Schiffer Publishing, Ltd.
4880 Lower Valley Road
Atglen, PA 19310
Phone: (610) 593-1777; Fax: (610) 593-2002
E-mail: Info@schifferbooks.com

For our complete selection of fine books on this and related subjects, please visit our website at www.schifferbooks.com. You may also write for a free catalog.

This book may be purchased from the publisher. Please try your bookstore first.

We are always looking for people to write books on new and related subjects. If you have an idea for a book, please contact us at proposals@schifferbooks.com.

Schiffer Publishing's titles are available at special discounts for bulk purchases for sales promotions or premiums. Special editions, including personalized covers, corporate imprints, and excerpts can be created in large quantities for special needs. For more information, contact the publisher.

Designed by Stephanie Daugherty
Type set in Blackadder ITC/New Baskerville BT

ISBN: 978-0-7643- 3328-6
Printed in The United States of America

❧ Dedication ❧

This book is dedicated to all of the grassroots organizations, families, and individuals who are struggling to overcome innumerable hurdles in order to preserve our nation's past. I hope the ghostly tales and mysteries surrounding each of your sites continue to attract new visitors and further your efforts.

❧ Acknowledgments ❧

My sincerest thanks go out to everyone who contributed a ghostly encounter from these plantations, helped with historical details, guided me on tours and answered my endless questions, and endured the sweltering heat or freezing cold to grant me access to a site. Your kind contributions made this book possible.

Thank you, LeeAnne, for all of your help in scheduling and investigating. Your enthusiasm for paranormal research is unmatched and your love of history is contagious—keep passing it on.

Finally, I am grateful to my family for being so supportive of my efforts, no matter what the project. I couldn't do any of it without you!

❧ Contents ☙

⋙ Introduction ⋘

When one thinks of life in Colonial and Antebellum Virginia, the image of rolling fields of tobacco with a grand plantation home at the center often comes to mind. The planters who established these farms sought refuge from the geographical, religious, and social confinements of England. They found that the fertile lands near the rivers in the New World could produce bounties of nearly every crop planted, and many of the lower and middle classes were able to build fortunes here as a result. Virginia was truly the heart of the new "Land of Opportunity."

Sadly, much of that opportunity came with a dark moral shadow. Native Americans were driven out of their ancestral farmlands, sometimes in bloody battles. No matter how many attempts the Natives made to push back the invasion of Europeans, they were defeated by well-armed Colonists who grossly outnumbered them.

Another shadow was the introduction of human slavery in the Colonies by the Dutch. This turn in history was seen as the driving force of agriculture in the South. During a time when all field work was done by hand, each slave on a plantation was seen as a moneymaker – something to increase the farm's yields. Conditions were deplorable for the people kept in bondage, yet most endured the lifestyle forced upon them for fear of death.

Life in early Virginia was not easy for the majority who lived here. Their physical and emotional struggles seem to have left a deep imprint on the land, sort of a paranormal scar, which reappears now and again to remind us of those difficult years. When I set out to write this book, I found out quickly just how deeply some parts of that imprint were set.

Most of the plantations I chose to include here are ones I visited frequently on school field trips as a child, back in a time when one was thought rude to bring up the topic of ghosts in a historic location. Those same sites now have come to embrace their haunted reputations, and even view them as a way to encourage tourists to experience some of the history that is still active today – through their ghosts.

Some of the plantations here I had never heard of, much less paid a visit to, until this project came about. I'm very pleased that

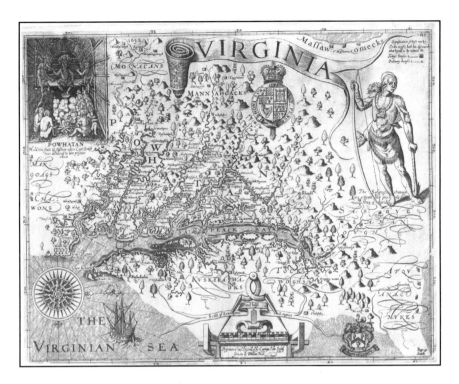

those places found me when they did, as every one offered a distinct look into the past and had ghostly activity as unique as the farms themselves.

During my solo field investigations of these historic sites, I employed only basic equipment – a camera, digital audio recorder, tape recorder, and video camera – which varied depending on the limitations set by each plantation. These investigations are not meant to be considered a determining factor of the legitimacy of paranormal encounters reported at a location. Instead, they were intended to provide a quick snapshot of the level of activity *during the time of the investigation*. Spirits do not always make their presence known while a researcher is onsite.

While I had hoped to visit and investigate all of the old Virginia farms included here, there were a few that were closed for archeological field work or restoration. The tales of paranormal happenings at those plantations, however, were so compelling (or in some cases bizarre) that I felt the need to share their stories with you regardless. I hope you are as intrigued by the reports of phantom fireballs and apprehensive apparitions as I am, and I urge you to set out and visit those sites when they reopen their doors.

Early Virginia:
Eastern Plantations

❧ Rosewell ❧

A plantation truly like no other in Virginia is Rosewell, former home of the Page family, in beautiful Gloucester County. The magnificent home was ruined by fire in 1916, but still provides a unique look at the rise and fall of members of one of Virginia's most prominent families. When I laid eyes on Rosewell, I found it obvious why the site had inspired so many supernatural legends.

Rosewell's construction is thought to have been completed sometime around 1725. The home appeared much more like a proper English manor house than any of its colonial cousins. Mann Page established his plantation, dubbed "the finest in all of Virginia" upon its completion, near the convergence of the York River and Carter's Creek. His choice of location was likely more politically focused than due to the beauty of the countryside. Robert "King" Carter lived nearby and would form close and influential ties to the Page family who moved in practically next door.

Instead of Rosewell welcoming its new residents in joy, the occasion was a melancholy one. Page's manor was finished only a very short time before his death. Historians tell that he was laid out for funeral display in the plantation's grand hall before the family was even able to move in.

Mann Page's impressive estate was passed to his son, Mann Page II, along with the enormous debt his father had secretly amassed to complete the construction. Mann II used the home's grandeur to help build a circle of friends in high places. The younger Page and his new family lived at Rosewell behind the guise of prosperity while the burden of debt slowly chipped away at his health. Upon the death of Mann II, Rosewell was again passed along Page family lines, and continued in that tradition until the home was sold out of the family in the mid-nineteenth century.

The site seemed to carry a dark cloud for centuries and it was only fitting that a place attached to so much turmoil and tragedy would prompt legends of otherworldly influence. Rosewell's earliest recorded tale of a resident spirit was alluded to by Lucy Burwell Page Saunders in her story, "Leonora and the Ghost." The main character, Leonora, heard clanking and heavy footsteps on the stairs late one Christmas Eve. When she arose to investigate the sounds, she saw the carriage driver eating the Christmas feast in the Grand

Hall, and mistook him for a ghost. Several evenings of clanking and footsteps eventually led to local men staying overnight to try and find the cause of the disturbance. The noises were quickly discovered to be the nightly antics of a family of packrats.

While this story of a young girl with a colorful imagination is lighthearted and amusing, a piece of history woven into the tale is quite dark. Lucy tells of a runaway slave who was captured nearby and held overnight in Rosewell's Blue Room – quarters thought to harbor the restless souls somehow connected to a funeral pall stored in a trunk there. The man was mysteriously found dead the following morning. His death was likely due to intentional mistreatment or internal injuries suffered during his capture, but it only proved to heighten the fear and superstition surrounding the Blue Room. Residents avoided it whenever possible, but it is said that Thomas Jefferson locked himself away in the Blue Room to draft part of the Declaration of Independence while visiting in 1776.

The spirits of former slaves at Rosewell are said to have made their reappearance in the early twentieth century. Neighbors of the manor were known to visit the ruin and gawk at the shell of the home destroyed by fire just a few years earlier. One local legend claims that a family visiting near dusk one autumn day heard a group of voices singing an old tune often sung by slaves returning from the fields. Unable to locate the source of the sound, they fled. Similar accounts have been reported dozens of times in the decades since.

I ventured to Rosewell at the peak of summer's heat and humidity, which seemed somehow amplified in Gloucester County's coastal areas. Brown signs directed me down the rural highways and through the country back roads without any question of my accuracy. A long dirt driveway sandwiched between thick, dark woods and a spooky cornfield led me to the Rosewell visitor center and archaeology lab.

Hilarie, the Executive Director of Rosewell, greeted me in the gift shop and was happy to share her own version of the ghost story connected to the Page family estate that was featured in L.B. Taylor's *Ghosts of Tidewater*. She explained that many years ago, a couple visited the ruin and spotted an old car on the grounds. As they remarked how unusual it was to find the car out near the unoccupied property, they claimed to see a woman suddenly appear in the driver's seat. Startled and frightened, the couple drove off believing that they'd seen a ghost.

It took the two a few minutes to gather their wits and calm down. Once they had, they decided to go back to the ruin and investigate. When they approached Rosewell, the car and the woman had vanished.

"I know this story is the real thing," Hilarie said with a wink, "because it was told to me by the woman in the old car."

A relative of the property's caretaker lived nearby and would often park her car at Rosewell to discourage trespassers. She had just

arrived when the couple came for their visit and she didn't want them to see her walk home and leave the car. Her solution was to duck down behind the dash until they left. She was spotted when she raised her head to check if the couple was still there. Once they sped off, she decided it was probably best to drive home that night. That explained why the couple found to trace of an old car or ghostly woman upon their return.

Hilarie pointed me towards the center's exhibit room where I explored cases of artifacts uncovered at the manor site. There were many spectacular photos of Rosewell before fire claimed the interior and roof. Also displayed was a very detailed model of Rosewell as it was originally designed – before renovations, alterations, and its eventual destruction.

Hilarie informed me that there were some volunteers working on the ruin and that, if I hurried, I might be able to find out if they had any ghostly encounters to share. I didn't miss a beat.

The short drive from the visitor center to Rosewell was like a trip back through time. I left a modern archeology lab and museum, rounded a bend, and found myself staring at what resembled a dilapidated castle in miniature.

What Rosewell had lost in architectural beauty, it had certainly gained in sculptural appeal. Tall brick stalagmites, formerly parts of the exterior walls of the house and its chimneys, stood with rugged, crumbling edges, and their tops supporting only sky. I could still make out several window openings, a doorway, and a huge set of stairs that once led to the grand entrance. Fireplaces suspended

A glimpse of Rosewell before it was destroyed by fire in 1916.

The ruins of the once majestic manor house are now being stabilized and preserved.

twenty and thirty feet above ground added to the spooky, surreal atmosphere.

I met two men on the site who were tackling bits of the neverending job of stabilizing what remained of the standing brick and mortar. The older of the pair told me he'd been working on Rosewell for well over a decade. I was hoping he'd have some unusual experiences to share from that stretch of service, but when I brought up the subject of ghosts, both men bristled. The young helper feigned needing something from the truck to avoid the discussion. Something was definitely "off" there and I didn't need to be Nancy Drew to figure that out.

After some meandering around the topic for a bit, the older man finally said, "In all my time here I've never seen anything, but I'll tell you, I never felt alone either." He then quickly changed the subject and told me a colorful story about a snake that would come out just to listen to his friend sing while he worked. I made a mental note to save any singing until I was safely in the car, and set out to have a look around.

I explored the site for a while, poking my head into old fireplaces and climbing giant mounds of brick and sand to get better photos. The two workmen shouted a good-bye from their truck and rumbled off down the old road, leaving me at Rosewell alone. I couldn't help but think of one of the most mysterious ghost stories of the plantation once I got used to my solitude – the Lady in Red. No one is really sure who she is or why she supposedly haunts Rosewell, but many witnesses claim to have seen her coming down the stairs opposite the river and running off into the nearby woods. I made sure to snap more photos than I thought necessary of those crumbling steps.

Behind the old stairs I found a well-preserved brick cellar. It appeared to be the only portion of the house that still had its walls and ceiling intact, likely thanks to its arched-top design. The doorway to the cellar was partially blocked by a pile of rubble and the opening was too small to pass through without crawling. Remembering that wildlife was very likely to be seeking refuge from Virginia's oppressive

A surreal look at suspended second and third story fireplaces is only one of the experiences unique to Rosewell.

July heat in there, I opted to instead shoot my photos through what remained of the door. After snapping about a dozen pictures, my camera decided it needed a break and refused to process or save any more images. I moved about five feet away from the cellar door onto more stable ground to try and determine the cause of the camera's failure. All of my tests showed that it was in perfect working order – full batteries and plenty of memory space. I went back to the cellar opening for another try. Nothing – no shutter snap, no flash, nada. Growing both curious and frustrated, I backed off and checked the camera again. I took three photos in a row with no ill effects. My third attempt to photograph the cellar was met with no problems.

The heat began to wear on me, so I decided to explore the trail that led into the shade of the nearby woods. About 100 yards into the trees and atop a slight hill, I discovered a huge brick cistern. The debris that dotted the bottom was covered in such a thick layer of moss that every object's true identity was unrecognizable. I had taken several photos of the enormous sunken cylinder when "the feeling" hit me – someone or something was watching me. Every hair on my neck stood on end as a chill cut through the dense humidity. I had the unsettling thought that something could easily give me a tiny shove and I'd be helpless to prevent tumbling into the pit before me.

The arch-topped cellar where an unexplained camera malfunction added to the mysteries of the day.

I calmed my nerves and opened my senses to the forest. No birds sang to one another and I could not make out even the tiny buzz of an insect. Just then, a rustling only a few yards away gave me a

start, and a stealthy squirrel shot up a nearby tree. Was that what I'd been sensing that had me on full alert? Instead of dwelling on the thought, I headed back to the ruin for a quick lunch.

I found a cozy picnic table tucked between two towering black walnut trees only a few feet from the woods I had just left. Taking in the peace and quiet of the Gloucester countryside, I noticed the feeling I was being watched slowly creep over me again. I tried my best to ignore the weighty

An enormous brick cistern sits in the dense woodland behind the ruins.

sensation while I finished my meal. Now I understand fully what the workman meant when he said he never really felt alone here.

I collected my things, relieved to move a little farther from the trees, and ventured to the old cemetery plot to collect more photos. According to a stone marker at the site, the bodies in the family graveyard had been relocated to the Abingdon Church on nearby Route 17 many decades earlier. The plot still gave off that "cemetery" feeling that made me wonder if only *some* of the bodies had been moved. There was always the possibility that some graves were not marked or recorded and their occupants still lay at Rosewell. My camera clicked away.

Satisfied with my collection from the day and completely exhausted from the weather, I returned home to take a closer look at the images I captured.

Rosewell looked almost magical in photos. I've never encountered any place like it before, and having the opportunity to climb around in the rubble only made it feel more mysterious. I combed through each image, careful not to be swept away by the beauty of the scenes, and discovered that many of them contained unidentified blurs and orbs. Four photos especially grabbed hold of my attention – they were taken in the darkness of the cellar without the assistance of a flash. My camera's light sensitivity was set at its highest capability, and it managed to record several shots in succession showing a large, bright orb that appeared to travel from the left side of the cellar to the right. These four photos were those that immediately preceded my strange camera malfunction.

My experiences at Rosewell were mixed – I felt curious, excited, adventurous, and, as you know, a little spooked. The photos I collected allow me now to relive every one of those sensations over and over. Did I see the mysterious Lady in Red or hear the spectral song of slaves returning from the fields? No. Did I bring home "proof" of the paranormal at Rosewell? Maybe. What I did encounter, though, was a unique look at part of Virginia's haunting history even more exhilarating than the old legends could convey.

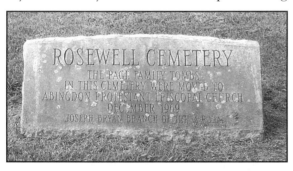

All that is left of the family cemetery is a marker that tells where all the remains have been moved.

❧ Adam Thoroughgood House ❧

$\mathcal{T}$ucked away in a modern residential neighborhood in the sunny coastal town of Virginia Beach, a curious tourist can find a seventeenth century hidden treasure – complete with ghosts.

Overlooking the Lynnhaven River, only a mile and a half from its point of entry to the Atlantic Ocean, sits the Thoroughgood Plantation. Its namesake, Adam Thoroughgood, was born in Norfolk, England, and came to Virginia as an indentured servant. After fulfilling his indenture, he worked diligently at establishing his place in the Colony. He obtained the tract of land in 1636 on which his family home now stands, and was elected to serve in the House of Burgesses soon after. Eventually, Thoroughgood served on the Governor's Council as a Justice of the Court and was Captain of the local militia. His climb in social status, however, apparently took a toll on his health. Thoroughgood died at age 36.

Historians believe that the house at the Thoroughgood Plantation was built by Adam's grandson, Argoll, in 1680. It is one of the oldest brick homes in the United States today. The estate has long since passed out of the Thoroughgood family and is now in the care of the City of Virginia Beach and the private citizens who raise funds for its preservation. The site opened as an interpretive museum of seventeenth century colonial life soon after its restoration in the late 1950s. Since that time, visitors and volunteers have witnessed a variety of unexplained events attributed to the spirits of two Thoroughgood descendents.

Residents of the Thoroughgood subdivision that surrounds the estate, claim to have seen a woman carrying a candle inside the house, going about what appeared to be "business as usual." As recently as the spring of 2008, a group of visiting school children, with no prior knowledge of the apparitions there, reported seeing a woman in a white gown walking near the window with a candle. When they asked their chaperone why the woman had a candle in the daytime, she vanished.

The mystery woman of the Thoroughgood House has a companion that is most often witnessed walking the halls of the home. Both tourists and staff have reported seeing a man in a brown vest and knee pants. When spoken to, the man seems unaware of those addressing him. The guides at the museum believe this wandering spirit is that of Argoll Thoroughgood.

One of the most startling events known to take place at the estate was witnessed by a group of nearly thirty tourists and a volunteer docent. The group entered the dining room while the docent continued sharing her prepared facts for the tour. Suddenly, four glass hurricane globes rose from around their candles, moved several inches out into the room, and simultaneously crashed onto the floor. Rumor has it the volunteer guide has not been back since.

In addition to these apparitions and amazing poltergeist activity, staff of the museum note that the house is seldom quiet – especially when it is empty. The sound of muffled footsteps, faint voices, and mysterious knocks are so regular that they occur almost every day. Furniture has even been found pushed against the walls on the second floor of the house upon employees' arrival in the mornings. No one has found any logical or natural explanation for any of these phenomena.

Could the restless spirits at the Thoroughgood House remain so energetic because of their close proximity to the powerful currents of the Lynnhaven River and the Atlantic Ocean? Perhaps they are simply happy to share with guests a more *authentic* look at Colonial life in Virginia.

The Adam Thoroughgood House in Virginia Beach. LOC Call Number: HABS VA, 77-LYNHA.V, 1-3.

❧ Bacon's Castle ❧

The Arthur Allen House in Surry County is one of very few surviving seventeenth-century structures in Virginia. Its interesting architecture, historical significance, and tales of bizarre paranormal activity make it the most unusual plantation on the James River.

First, to clarify things, the grand brick structure is not actually a castle, nor does it have anything to do with pork. The house was built by Arthur Allen and was completed sometime near 1665. Arthur died only four years after moving into his manor, but the property was passed on to his son, Arthur II. Arthur II enjoyed several years as a member of the Virginia House of Burgesses while residing in Surry, and is said to have lavished great attention on his family home.

During this prosperous period for Arthur II, Nathaniel Bacon, a planter from Curles' Neck Plantation (about thirty miles upriver from the Allen House), was organizing a rebellion against the Royal Governor of Virginia, William Berkeley, for his "tolerance" of the Native Americans in the area. Bacon believed that the natives should be driven out and the land made available to colonial farmers, but Berkeley was fond of negotiating peacefully with local tribes. The Rebellion attacked a Susquehannock village, who later retaliated by attacking plantations and killing sixty settlers.

In an attempt to avoid a large-scale war with the natives, Governor Berkeley set out to suppress Bacon and his followers. Members of the Rebellion seized Arthur Allen's home in September of 1676, fortified it much like a castle of the old country, and made a stand there against Government Loyalists. Their stand lasted until December of that same year. Governor Berkeley's men captured the "fort" and used it to fend off further advances from the Rebellion, which finally died out about a month later.

Williamsburg's *Virginia Gazette* newspaper made the first mention of the new nickname of Allen's brick house in 1769: Bacon's Castle. The name stuck.

Bacon's Castle today is managed by the Association of the Preservation of Virginia Antiquities (APVA). Under their supervision, the 350-year old home has undergone extensive restoration and is now operated as a museum.

A riverside view of Bacon's Castle in the mid-twentieth century. LOC Call Number: HABS VA, 91-SURRY.V, 1-34.

There are two things visitors to the Castle ask about more than any other. First, they want to know about the unusual, twisted triple-chimneys at the ends of the house. Then they want to know which chimney the ghostly fireball enters. You read that correctly. One of the strangest paranormal legends in Virginia concerns a glowing sphere that is said to come through the woods from the nearby cemetery, circle the house, and disappear down one of its chimneys. Others claim that the sphere merely floats near the rooftop of the house before returning to the graveyard where it originated. Tales of the fiery manifestation, the sight of which was interpreted as a bad omen for the witness, date back nearly three hundred years.

Several individuals report having seen the fireball at varying intervals throughout history, but their stories are today overshadowed by a truly remarkable account in 1930. A local church revival session was host to dozens who together watched the infamous sphere for several seconds – until it vanished through the woods, heading towards Bacon's Castle!

While no one is certain of the origin of this unusual apparition, legends, of course, have cropped up to offer an explanation. One popular story is that the fireball is an earthbound reminder of a comet that was visible over Virginia in 1675 and was thought to be

A red fireball is said to circle the house and descend one of its chimneys. LOC Call Number: HABS VA, 91-SURRY.V, 1-33.

an ominous warning for the Colonies about Nathaniel Bacon and his bloody rebellion. Another legend tells of a servant who was less than punctual with the completion of his duties for the day. When he was coming back towards the Castle from the fields, a mass of flames overcame him and burned him to death. While it is more likely that the man accidentally set fire to his clothing with his lantern, the legend is retold as a reminder to keep one's "nose to the grindstone."

The stories of the astounding fireball are not the only ghostly tales surrounding Bacon's Castle. Since the APVA acquired the property in the 1970s, many live-in curators have made claims of unexplained sights and sounds there. One tale, made famous by L.B. Taylor in his *The Ghosts of Tidewater*, describes a curator awakened in the middle of the night by the sound of his toddler son laughing in his crib. When he went to investigate, he found his son wide awake and asking for "the lady with the white hands" who had been tickling him. While unnerving, a toddler-tickling ghost seems to be a dramatic improvement over a ball of flames.

A visiting preacher witnessed a parlor door open after hearing phantom footsteps on the stairs and in the hall. LOC Call Number: HABS VA, 91-SURRY.V, 1-17.

Probably the spookiest story from a museum employee is another that was shared by Taylor. A guide was preparing for her first tour of the day when someone unseen ran through the hall in which she was standing. She claims to have heard the footfalls of the entity and even felt something brush her sleeve. The guide was surprised, but not scared away. She had already heard some of the things that others, like Mrs. Warren, had witnessed.

Mrs. Charles Walker Warren owned Bacon's Castle in the early twentieth century. She was hosting a visiting Baptist preacher who claimed that he heard "someone" come down the stairs from the second floor just before the parlor door opened and a breeze brushed past him. Though he never saw anyone, he was quite convinced a presence was there when a rocking chair across the room began to move like someone had sat down.

Mrs. Warren herself reported that, on a separate occasion, a large dictionary was thrown across a room by unseen hands and the heavy iron stand on which the dictionary normally stood was tossed into a corner. Unable to find a logical explanation for the events, Mrs. Warren was comfortable attributing the activity she witnessed, as well as the encounter of the visiting preacher, to the ghosts of Bacon's Castle.

Strange sights, sounds, and objects moving without assistance from the living are still common phenomena at the Arthur Allen House. Some Surry residents still claim to see the mysterious fireball on occasion. If you're like many lucky tourists to the historic home, your visit to Bacon's Castle may even include a bit of that paranormal activity along with your tour.

❧ Endview ❧

A jewel of preservation sits on the outer edge of the City of Newport News, a historic water town near the Chesapeake Bay. Positioned on the peninsula formed by the York and James Rivers, a tract of land established in 1626 by the Harwood family is now the site of the Harwood Plantation house, built in 1769.

The simple white clapboard house, which architectural enthusiasts call "Georgian-Inspired," was constructed only about a hundred yards from a freshwater spring. Vast expanses of fertile farmland surrounded it. It was no wonder the site had been favored by Native Americans for over a thousand years before English settlement.

The plantation home was passed through direct lineage in the Harwood family until it was purchased by a more distant relative, Dr. Humphrey Harwood Curtis, in 1856. The doctor and his young wife took up residence and soon renamed the estate "Endview Plantation" because of its peculiar perpendicular alignment to the nearby Yorktown Road. Dr. Curtis established a successful medical practice at Endview and watched his farm flourish until 1861, when the Civil War came to Newport News and McClellan's Peninsula Campaign forced the family to evacuate their home for Danville, Virginia.

In the Curtis' absence, Endview was used briefly by defending Confederate forces as a field hospital for the sick and wounded. After the Confederate retreat, the Union army seized Endview and relocated seven former slave families there to live and work. Dr. Curtis, unlike many Virginia farm owners, successfully regained ownership rights to his property after the end of the war in 1865. He went back to practicing medicine at Endview until his death in 1881.

The plantation remained in the hands of Dr. Curtis' heirs for over a century after his passing. The family sold the historic site to the City of Newport News in 1985, ending over 300 years of Harwood-Curtis occupation of Endview. The fact that the home remained in the same lineage for so long is not only a rare occurrence, but probably the most likely reason for its well-preserved condition. A lived-in house generally sees a much slower rate of deterioration than an abandoned one.

Endview today serves as a museum and Civil War education center. I was amazed to learn on my visit there that, even though oral, photographic, and written records were passed along in the family, some mysteries still surrounded the estate. A large exploratory archeological dig had been launched to try and find some of the manor's original dependencies. No one knew the location of the all-important kitchen just a hundred years after it was last seen. It was startling to see how quickly the past could be lost with no one looking out for it.

But local accounts claim that there is someone looking out for Endview. An apparition, dubbed "The Woman in White" because of her luminous white gown, has been reported by passersby on the adjacent highway, visitors to the home, participants in Civil War re-enactments and encampments on the grounds, and employees of the museum. Those who told of catching a glimpse of the woman all say she seemed at ease, perhaps deep in thought. I hoped to find out more about this pensive spirit and maybe even bring home a piece of evidence in support of the legend.

My visit to Endview coincided with an ominous looking storm rolling over the horizon. The dark clouds occasionally let through a few bright rays of sunlight that gave the grounds a surreal, dreamlike feel. My timing could not have been better. I circled the main house, photographing it from every angle, and then ventured to its rustic little outbuildings. On my way to the old dairy shed, a tiny family cemetery bound by a white picket fence caught my eye as a good place to leave an audio recorder. I leaned over the short pickets and tucked the device in the grass near the foot of one of the cemetery's two graves. Before walking away, I was sure to announce my interest in hearing from any spirits that might be present.

I continued my photographic exploration of Endview's grounds until the darkening clouds prompted me to get on to touring the interior. As if on cue, a guide rounded the corner of the house just as I approached the basement entrance.

Endview Plantation in Newport News.

A tiny family cemetery with the graves of a mother and child lies beside the house.

My tour of Endview began in a museum-like exhibit under the home's low cellar ceiling. On display were photos of Dr. Curtis and his family, along with several glass and rusty metal artifacts discovered on the property over the preceding decades. Jim, my guide, then led me up a steep and narrow staircase to the first floor. There I examined a recreation of the doctor's medical office (in what used to be the dining room, of all things) and lingered for a bit in the family's cozy parlor. The home was furnished with simple period pieces and seemed to reflect the no-nonsense mindset of a man of business.

We continued to the second floor where I was shown two spacious bedrooms, one for the children and the other for the parents, and a small third room that was added at an unknown time. Yet another of Endview's mysteries. Among the items on the second floor were a large tin portrait of Humphrey Harwood Curtis' sister, Francis, and a dressing box that had belonged to her. Jim explained that Francis had died very young and it was speculated that she may be the apparition so often seen on the property. I thought Francis was quite lovely and would make for a pleasant spirit to encounter; maybe that's why no one who reported seeing her was especially shaken afterwards.

Another member of the staff later recounted to me a story that made me question whether the specter was in fact Maria Curtis, and not her sister-in-law. During an open house at Endview, a visitor was admiring some nineteenth-century baby clothing lain out on an upstairs bed. When she turned to leave the room, she claimed to have seen an older woman standing opposite her. A few minutes later, the visitor saw a portrait of Maria in the parlor and exclaimed to a docent that she'd just seen that woman upstairs. The docent never saw a woman fitting the description the visitor gave her enter or leave the house.

Jim and I moved out onto the front porch and I asked if he'd ever seen the Woman in White himself. "No, but I've experienced some other strange things in the house," he said. "I've been closing up and counting out the register in the basement when I heard someone walking around on the first floor. At first I thought I'd left a door unlocked and a guest had come in, but when I went up to check, I found everything locked up. There was no one in the house."

Jim went on to tell me that he wasn't alone in hearing the phantom footsteps; several other museum employees had reported similar encounters. On more than one occasion, guides closing out the day's receipts in the basement reported music coming from the first floor, along with the more common footsteps. Again, when they went to investigate, they found the house empty. A non-functioning melodeon sits in the parlor where the music was thought to have emanated.

Other unexplained happenings in the house have been reported by staff, but these things were neither sights nor sounds. Intense smells of cooking have been detected inside the home during the early morning hours before the museum opens to the public. The scents noted were very specific: perked coffee, roast beef, yeast bread, and biscuits. Historians made mention of Maria's love to cook and her regular hosting of Confederate Veterans for Sunday dinner, both before and after her husband's death. Is she continuing the tradition in the afterlife? There is no kitchen in the house to account for the mysterious, albeit delicious, odors.

I was about to retrieve my audio recorder and leave when Jim asked, "Did you visit the family cemetery?" He was pointing to the woods on the other side of a tiny footbridge near the spring. To my surprise, there were more than just the two lonely graves near the house. A Harwood family plot, thought to date from the seventeenth century, lay just uphill from the manor. Jim gave me directions and I headed for the bridge.

My short walk through the woods was a strange one. About a dozen or so yards down the trail, I noticed that the trees around me seemed to change. What would normally be straight pines, tall oaks, and stately maples were instead a strange mass of gnarled and twisted trunks. The closer I came to the cemetery, the more unusual the surroundings appeared – the forest looked as though the trees were slowly trying to crawl away.

I found a small collection of grave markers in a clearing under several bent Black Walnut trees. It was easy to see from the numerous mounds and rectangular depressions in the soil that there were far more Harwoods buried there than the stones indicated. I collected dozens of photos from the site before sitting down to listen and observe my surroundings more closely. No birds sang, no crickets chirped. The only noise was the occasional breeze rustling the treetops and a distant rumble of thunder. Fall thunderstorms in Virginia are a very unusual occurrence, and listening to one approach while sitting in a graveyard under trees that looked like they were about to rearrange themselves made my heart pound. I wasn't consciously *afraid* of anything, but I found myself rethinking my trip up the path.

I managed to hold out another five minutes or so before a sudden, loud clap of thunder prompted my return to the manor house. I collected my audio recorder from the little graveyard and snapped a few more photos before heading back to the parking lot, and to the twenty-first century.

Strange, twisted woods surrounded the old Harwood Cemetery.

Though there were only a few stones visible, it was obvious there were many more graves than were marked.

Reviewing the photographs I took from Endview was like looking at careful recreations of Currier and Ives paintings – each seemed to capture the quiet essence of farm life. I flipped through about six images of the front of the manor house, taken one after another, when I spotted something unusual on a second floor window. I pulled out a magnifying glass, zoomed in on the *Something*, and pondered the possibilities. Whatever the little Something was, it was moving *very* quickly and seemed to have a W-shape. The photos seconds before and after the suspect shot revealed nothing out of the ordinary. My first thought was that I'd simply been fooled by a sneaky moth, but other photos from the day that captured insects showed them frozen and still – not blurred like this mystery object. The second thing to enter my mind was a strangely similar image I captured at Appomattox Manor a year earlier, one that was later nicknamed "The Fairy Photo" by the first experts to examine it. After that, I wasn't really sure what to think.

Since there were no other anomalous photos from Endview with which to compare this oddity, I decided to review the audio recording in search of answers. The sound of the breeze rustling the magnolia leaves and the soft rumble of thunder brought back the heightened sense of alertness I'd felt while sitting in the old Harwood family graveyard in the woods. About twenty minutes into the track, I was startled by a distinct "tap, tap" on the recorder. Had a bird come to inspect the device I'd so carefully hidden in the grass? I amplified the moments before and after the tapping in hopes of hearing the flap of a set of wings or an animal moving in the leaves. There was nothing but silence. I listened further, but could detect no natural culprit who may have caused the taps.

I passed the recording on to several other paranormal investigators for their thoughts, without first telling them the

A strange anomaly was discovered in front of the center window on the second floor.

conditions surrounding the placement of the device or what I thought I'd captured. Every investigator came back to me with the same report – they heard no voices, but someone knocked on the recorder. All presumed it had been me because the sounds were so clear and loud. Only after they shared their opinions did I let them know that I was nowhere near when the tapping occurred.

There is no doubt in my mind that a variety of mysterious events are taking place at Endview Plantation. Each witness to the site's strange occurrences is completely convinced that what they experienced, whether they were sights, sounds, or smells, was not a product of their imagination. While I had no personal paranormal encounters during my visit to the historic farm, I did come away with two very interesting (and still unexplained) pieces of data that have only served to fan the flames of my curiosity regarding the existence of supernatural activity there.

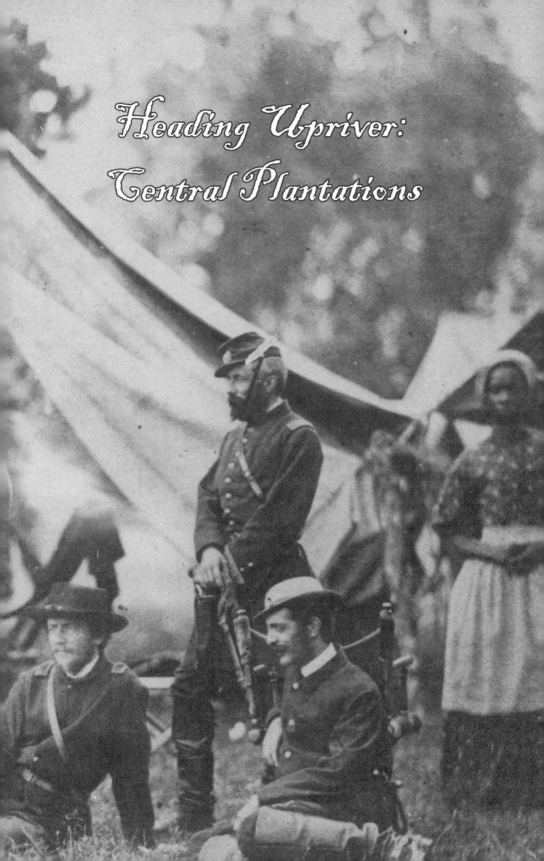

Heading Upriver:
Central Plantations

༄ Shirley ༄

surreal drive through cotton fields and past crumbling slave quarters led me to a proper four-square plantation house. Long dirt roads seem to take a visitor back in time in many places in Charles City County, and the roads that end at Shirley are a prime example.

The land on which Shirley stands was part of one of the earliest royal patents in the colonies in 1613. Today, it boasts the title of the oldest family-owned business in North America, thanks to the eleven generations of the Carter-Hill family who have kept it in operation as a working farm. Could the stability of Shirley Plantation and its strong family ties be the reasons spirits would want to cling there? I hoped to find out.

My tour of the plantation offered an up-close view of the details of the home that weren't included in any of the history books I had read. The first thing that struck me as unusual was the elaborate

Shirley Plantation has been a working farm for nearly 300 years.

The brick dovecote was an indicator of the wealth and social status of the Carter-Hill family.

dovecote at the center of the parking lot. This small, cylindrical brick building was an unquestionable symbol of the family's wealth and social status. Squib, or roasted dove, was considered an eighteenth-century delicacy, and anyone with such a dovecote would have been quite the epicurean.

The second thing that caught my eye was the formal symmetry of the buildings and the landscape. The balanced layout of the property felt very English in design, more so than the other early plantations of the area.

Something else I noticed gave me a slight uneasy feeling – the doors to the main house had no knobs. The only way to gain entrance to the home was with the huge master key. Was this a precautionary measure against intruders? Did the Hills who had the house constructed in 1738 fear an attack from Indians or possibly the slaves who worked the farm? It was a frightening thought, but both scenarios were likely.

Inside of Shirley's grand main house, I was treated to a view of the home's famous "floating staircase," an impressive architectural accomplishment of the eighteenth century. The staircase appeared to have no support at all, but its structural stability came from hidden iron fastenings secured to the thick brick exterior walls.

My guide, John, escorted me through the central hall, parlor, dining room, and finally – to the bedroom of Aunt Pratt. "Aunt Pratt" was actually Martha Hill Pratt, a relative of the Hill family who never actually lived at Shirley. Her portrait, however, has

The buildings and grounds of the estate are arranged in a formal English design.

hung there for centuries and, according to the plantation's most fantastic legend, has no desire to leave.

The tale that has been passed down through the generations is that Pratt's portrait hung on the first floor for decades without incident. During a period of redecorating, the painting was moved to a second floor bedroom. The night it was hung in its new location, the family was awakened by the sounds of the portrait banging

violently against the wall. Afraid to dispose of it for fear of a spirit's vengeance, the Hills decided to move the painting to the attic. The following night, so much noise and clatter came from the attic that no one could rest. The family finally resorted to hanging Pratt back in her original spot on the first floor.

Peace returned to the home, but Aunt Pratt was only appeased temporarily. Her portrait was sent to New York City in 1974 to be included in an exhibition of artifacts that were connected to psychic phenomena. Curators and visitors witnessed the painting vibrating and shaking in its display case and decided to place it in a museum storage locker before it was damaged or damaged anything exhibited with it. The following morning, guards discovered the portrait on the floor near the storage room door with its frame broken. Had Aunt Pratt attempted an escape? Some thought so. The events surrounding her stay in New York were witnessed by so many people and were so peculiar that Pratt was featured on the NBC's *Nightly News*.

The painting was returned to Virginia soon after it was found damaged. Its first stop was at a museum frame shop in Richmond where it stayed for repairs. The entire time Aunt Pratt's portrait was in the possession of the framer, he claimed that he heard bells every evening coming from the room in which it was stored. There were no bells in the building.

Pratt was quickly returned to Shirley, hung in her preferred location, and her noisy nights ended. Though the Carters who reside at Shirley today claim to hear frequent knocks and bangs in the home at night, none appear to come from Aunt Pratt.

I must admit that I was a little star-struck when I first saw the portrait. Martha was a fair-skinned brunette with serious eyes and a strong mouth. Since photography was not allowed in the main house, I placed my hopes on my beloved audio recorder to pick up any hint that the legend may be something more.

I recorded the entire tour, and for the first twenty minutes or so of my reviewing the data, heard only the voices of the guide, John, and the couple from South Carolina who accompanied me through the house. John's voice was occasionally interrupted by the sound of him unlocking a door or the echo of our footsteps as we moved from room to room. Then there was something else.

Near the end of the tour, in the bedroom where Aunt Pratt's portrait hangs, I captured a faint feminine whisper. The words lasted about three seconds, but all of my attempts to amplify the breathy sounds in hopes of understanding the message were fruitless. Could this have been the same spirit that caused such a fuss around that peculiar painting? I had no way to tell for certain, but I suspected there was some connection. Why was *this* room the only place the voice, or any strange sound for that matter, was captured?

Even though I was unable to use my camera inside of Shirley's main house, I snapped over a hundred shots elsewhere on the property. I hoped to find something in those photos that might help to validate the unusual audio recording and lend support to the legendary accounts of paranormal activity there. Strangely, the only visual disturbance in any of the photos was a tiny light spot in an image of the root cellar – all that remains of the former North flank of the main house after it was destroyed by fire.

Still, there was the whisper that kept nagging at my subconscious. Did Pratt have a message to convey that only modern technology could help to receive? If so, I hope the message offers some clue to why she is connected so strongly to her portrait. Maybe if that mystery is solved, Aunt Pratt can finally rest in peace.

≫ Berkeley ≪

*T*he most famous of all of Virginia's historic homes is Berkeley Plantation. The farm was established on part of a land grant in 1618 that was originally known as Berkeley Hundred. It seems as though the plantation's four centuries of occupation have been filled with sorrow. Visitors and employees of Berkeley believe that the home's many past tragedies have left deep wounds on the hearts of those who once lived there – those who are still believed to haunt the building and grounds.

Despite what you may have learned in grade school, Berkeley Plantation holds the honor of hosting the first Thanksgiving Feast in the New World in 1619. Colonists had settled in by that point and, much to the displeasure of local native tribes, were thriving. Berkeley's situation on a fertile outcrop on the north bank of the James River made the land ideal for agriculture. Farmers released

Berkeley Plantation, built in 1726 on the site of Berkeley Hundred. LOC Call Number: HABS VA, 19-CHARC.V, 4-19.

hogs into the wild, allowing them to forage and live off of the dense underbrush in the surrounding woodlands, and were rewarded with a generous brood for hunting in the harsh winter months. It appeared as though the bleak days of the early settlements were over, but not everyone was pleased with the colonists' good fortune.

The powerful Powhatan Confederacy, a part of the larger Algonquian Nation and tribe of the legendary chief Powhatan and his daughter, Pocahontas, was growing restless with the realization that the white settlers were not leaving. It seemed the English were instead quickly spreading deeper into territory revered by the natives. Powhatan's brother, a fierce warrior named Opechancanough, devised a plan to take the colonists by surprise.

On the morning of Good Friday, 1622, natives made a friendly and unarmed approach to plantations all across Virginia's Tidewater area. The colonists, lighthearted with the coming holidays, welcomed the natives into their homes and invited them to share their sermons and feasts. According to period accounts, the natives then simultaneously (and without any signal) took up the muskets standing in corners of rooms, knives at table settings, and any other weapon they could acquire. Nine colonists were brutally murdered at Berkeley, and an estimated one-third of the colonial settlement was slain in total.

The settlers did make an attempt to fight back against their native attackers. The majority of the survivors were not spared their lives; they won them in battle. The threat of other possible attacks hung over the colony like a dark cloud for decades.

Though it was difficult, the colonists at Berkeley Hundred were able to keep their claim to the plantation and only grew stronger and more confident with each successful harvest. Years passed and the estate flourished. The site eventually caught the eye of Benjamin Harrison IV in 1726, and a manor house was constructed with brick and mortar made from the surrounding landscape.

The plantation enjoyed many decades of prosperity. The Harrison family was very well known throughout the colonies and took great pride in their home.

Colonial Virginia, like the rest of the New World, began growing restless with British rule. Berkeley Plantation was thrown into the middle of this Revolutionary upheaval when Benedict Arnold arrived to arrest Benjamin Harrison V for treason. Luckily for Ben, he was training with the militia and missed Arnold's surprise visit. Berkeley, though, did not fare as well. Arnold is said to have had his men drag all of the furnishings, rugs, and artwork onto the lawn where they were then burned. The structure sustained little damage, but the family and servants present during the ordeal were bullied and terrified by Arnold and the accompanying troops. But, like their predecessors from the Berkeley Hundred plantation, the Harrisons bounced back and went on to call the estate home for many more generations.

Berkeley entered another period of flourish until it again crossed paths with a major event in American history in 1862 – The Civil War. General George McClellan's Peninsula Campaign rolled east toward Richmond, using the James River as its main highway, and found a convenient spot at "Harrison's Landing" to make camp. The General took Berkeley as his headquarters for a year, nearly destroying both the home and its farmland during his occupation. A diary account of an officer camped at Berkeley recalled how every tree, except an old poplar that shaded the kitchen, was cut down for firewood. The fine furniture of the plantation was again destroyed when it was dismantled and burned to keep troops warm during the blustery Virginia winter. The land was reduced to nothing but muddy red clay from all of the boots that stomped across it.

As though the hardship of hosting several thousand Union soldiers was not enough for the once-majestic farm, Berkeley and its dependency structures served as hospitals for several days to treat those severely wounded at the Battle of Malvern Hill, just a few miles to the east. Period writings claim that all of the home's expensive and exotic rugs had to be burned afterward because they were "ruined with copious amounts of blood and human gore." It appeared as though Berkeley had finally endured a tragedy so great that it would never recover.

Again, like a phoenix from the ashes, the plantation found a new start. It was purchased in 1907 by John Jamieson, a former drummer boy from McClellan's army, and decades of restoration and repair began. The care of Berkeley was later passed to John's son, Malcolm (Mac), and his wife, Grace. Though Mac and Grace passed away in the late 1990s, the estate remains in the hands of the Jamieson family.

Today, the kind staff at Berkeley welcomes visitors twelve months out of the year. They tell the tales of the home's past with such emotion that it's easy to forget that these guides in period costume were not *actually* there for these events.

I was delighted to travel to the plantation for a special evening tour with nearly forty other paranormal investigators. The staff granted me and the group's assistant organizer, Lee Anne, permission to set up several video cameras to film areas of the house during our visit. One was placed in part of the basement where employees had reported an

This image of the Fifth Army Corps was recorded early in their camp, only months before the grounds at Harrison's landing were stripped of trees. LOC Reference: LOT 4186, LC-USZ62-122103.

"uncomfortable" feeling, another in the southeast parlor on the ground floor, and the last in the southwest living room on the second floor. We started the cameras rolling and our investigation officially began.

Our hosts, Sue and Michelin, knew that we were all eager to hear about Berkeley's many ghosts and they did not fail to deliver. I switched on the audio recorder in my shirt pocket to capture their tales just in time. Peppered throughout their explanations of the home's history were stories about strange events they had experienced while working there. They recalled several loud thumps coming from the unoccupied second floor during the previous year's Spirit Tour, items such as a quill pen in the Gentleman's Room being rearranged when no one was there, catching glimpses of movement when they were alone in the house, and – most of all – the overwhelming feeling of a "presence" in nearly every room of the historic home. Sue explained that many alleged psychics had visited Berkeley and nearly all of them described the spirit of a child there.

"Personally," said Sue, "I think if anyone's haunting this house, it's Grace Jamieson. She *hated* the idea of having tours after five. I have no doubt that it was her making those banging sounds during the Spirit Tour – she probably wanted everyone out." I rolled the idea around in my head for a while. Would it be more likely that the spirit of someone who loved and cared for Berkeley would stick around after death than someone who died there tragically? Seeing as how Grace lived at the plantation for many decades and personally oversaw major restoration projects that resulted in the site's historic renaissance, it was a good chance she'd want to stay. She took great pride in her home and would want to make sure it was being properly treated and respected, even in spirit.

Berkeley's kitchen building lies only a few yards west of the main house.

We finished our guided tour of the house and were allowed to freely explore and investigate the grounds. The large group of attendees naturally broke up into smaller teams of four or five and set off collecting photographs and audio recordings. I stepped out through Berkeley's riverside entrance and paused to allow my teammates to catch up. My senses suddenly pricked and I felt the nagging stare of a stranger. I looked around and found no one. The feeling of watchful eyes grew heavier with every breath I took, and their gaze seemed to be coming from the kitchen building on Berkeley's west side. Instinctively, I turned and snapped a photo in that direction.

By that time, two of the people I was waiting for had joined me on the sidewalk. They were immediately alerted when the preview of the image I had just captured appeared in my camera's viewfinder. "What is *that*?" I exclaimed. There appeared to be a bright figure standing on the sidewalk in front of the kitchen. I had no idea exactly what I had captured, but I still had my wits about me and began popping off shot after shot of the kitchen building in hopes of recording something similar. My partners joined in, but we captured nothing else strange with our cameras.

Just as we decided that whatever I'd seen in my photo was not going to duplicate itself, an intense odor of cedar surrounded us. More investigators from our tour were exiting the plantation house and mentioned the strong aroma as soon as they passed through the doorway. The scent was so sharp and distinct that I thought perhaps a cedar tree nearby had been struck by lightning – but there was no sign of any type of weather disturbance, or a single cedar for that matter, as far as I could see. Within a minute, all traces of the odor disappeared.

I was curious and even a little stunned from the short series of events I'd just experienced when I headed toward the graveyard with the other members of my small team. Dusk was settling over the plantation. The deep shadows cast by the trees and shrubs bordering the winding path switched on some kind of primal awareness in all of us. Every rustling leaf or crunch of a twig under our feet registered as we neared our destination.

"Are we going the right way?" LeeAnne asked. "There haven't been any signs."

"I don't know for sure, but it feels right," I replied. It was a gut feeling that had been guiding me since we stepped away from the manor house. I felt like I was being led to the tiny graveyard by some kind of powerful magnet. Each turn in our route just seemed

The path that led to the graveyard was dark and shrouded by trees.

like the correct choice – and there were plenty of turns from which to choose. Mysteriously, we rounded a curve in the trail, climbed a gentle hill, and discovered the cemetery tucked in a small group of trees only a few yards ahead. Whatever had led us there made sure we weren't turned around in the fading light.

Ironically, the cemetery was cozy and calm compared to the rest of the spooky landscape. We noted some of the names on the gravestones and photographed each for our records. Several of us attempted to capture Electronic Voice Phenomena (EVP) on our digital recorders by asking questions of the entities we hoped were present. The air grew heavier and the feeling we were not alone became obvious to us all.

We finished collecting our photos and headed back towards the path to the manor house. We'd only walked a few yards when the sickeningly sweet odor of jasmine overcame us. Everyone stopped, sniffed, and exchanged suspicious glances. A few of us broke off from the path to search for a natural source of the floral scent we noted, some traveling as far as 100 feet away, but we found nothing. Strangely, the odor was only noticeable in that very short stretch of pathway. More photos and audio recordings were made at the area

The riverfront cemetery at Berkeley where the Harrison and Jamieson families rest.

of the phenomena, mostly to make note of the event, but also in hopes of capturing some other anomaly that would help support what many of us suspected – that the scent was caused by something supernatural.

Our walk back to the mansion was under a purple night sky dotted with glittering stars. The grounds were strangely silent aside from the crunch, crunch, crunch of our own footsteps. No crickets chirped. No brush stirred with foraging opossums or raccoons. No deer rustled the grass in the open fields. The peculiar lack of sounds in our surroundings gave me the uneasy feeling of someone watching us very closely from inside the trees just a few yards from the edge of the gravel path.

We followed the faint glow of light from the house and reached the back sidewalk in just a few minutes. LeeAnne stayed outside to find out if any of the other investigators had experienced anything unusual while exploring the grounds while I went in to break down our cameras and start packing the gear.

Our guide, Sue, took me into the off-limits second story to retrieve the equipment stationed there. The second and third floors had been the private living quarters of Mac and Grace Jamieson until

Grace and Mac Jamieson's private residence on the second floor is just as they left it. LOC Call Number: HABS VA, 19-CHARC.V, 4-29.

Grace's death in 1998. The place remained as she left it. I had the unwelcome sensation of intruding into someone's home as soon as we walked through the doorway that separated the main hall of the second floor from the stairway

I approached the video camera we had left about two hours earlier and prepared to shut it down. Peeking at the display screen on the device, I was puzzled to find it black and empty. I moved for a closer look and discovered that the two-stage power switch had been moved to the "off" position. The only way it could have been changed to that setting was by physically pressing the lock button while sliding the switch at the same time. This was no accident.

Curiosity had me completely in its grasp, so I turned on the camera to check the battery level and to see how much of the cassette had been used. My first thought was that someone had tampered with the camera for some reason, but I felt a tinge of comfort in the knowledge that the culprit couldn't have approached it without being caught in the camera's line of sight.

The camera powered up without hesitation and told me that it still had over one third of its battery power remaining. The two-hour cassette had only recorded eighty-three minutes of data. I made careful notes of my findings and made sure to ask Sue if anyone else had access to the second floor while we were out on the grounds. She assured me that it had been locked the entire time we were there and that she was the only one with the key.

This, the top of the list of the evening's odd events, had me scratching my head. I packed the video gear, grabbed a nearby audio recorder that had been set up to compliment the camera, and followed Sue to the hallway. "Thank you, Grace," she called into the empty rooms before locking the door.

We hurried to the southeast parlor to retrieve the next camera, an identical model to the one used upstairs. My jaw dropped when I discovered that this camera had also been switched off at some point during the evening. Again, tampering was my first suspicion, but the tripod had been tucked neatly into a corner with the lens capturing all of the room's entrances. No one could have approached it to stop the recording without being caught on film.

Just as I began breaking down the second camera, LeeAnne entered the parlor and stared at me in amazement as I described

A man's voice was captured in an audio recording during an investigation of the basement.

what I had found. She sped off for the basement to retrieve the third video camera, reappearing only moments later with gear in hand. Nothing unusual appeared to have happened to the third unit.

We were eager to review the tapes and see exactly who thought powering down our video equipment was entertaining. I took the camera that had been placed on the second floor and LeeAnne claimed the one from the first floor. We also each had several hours of audio evidence to review from a handful of audio recorders were had positioned in different areas of the mansion just before our tour. Still calling from the back of my mind was the photo I snapped on the sidewalk, and I was hardly able to contain my excitement at the thought of a closer inspection.

I drove home down the dark and winding Route 5, my heart pounding in my ears. My gut was telling me that with so many of us there collecting data, the likelihood of capturing something truly remarkable was high. I had no idea at the time how accurate my instinct was.

Upon viewing the tapes from the stopped video cameras, LeeAnne and I found that each recorded the same phenomena at roughly the same time. Nothing strange presented itself in the video and no one was seen or heard entering the rooms or approaching the cameras before the weirdness started. Each camera recorded a bit of "turbulence" when it appeared that they were attempting to focus on something close to the lens. Next came a slight wiggle in the frame, followed by a bright white screen with tiny flecks of black moving throughout. It looked similar to broadcast television static, but almost entirely white. The phenomena lasted several minutes and then the recordings were stopped. All of the tape beyond that point was black and untouched.

I had never seen anything like the results we captured with the video setup at Berkeley. Two cameras with the same anomaly on film and physically shut off by unknown means at nearly the same moment? Surely there must be a logical explanation, I thought. LeeAnne and I exhausted our wits, and those of the rest of the group, trying to find that explanation – we have yet to pinpoint it.

So, what about that photo that had me so puzzled? The "figure" I thought I saw was actually a light anomaly captured at what appeared to be a few yards from the kitchen house – a light anomaly like I have never seen in nearly two decades of my attempts at spirit photography. The glow of the object was so intense that it reminded me of the white-hot light of old magnesium flash bulbs. I would normally be quick to write off the finding as something in the environment

The "angelic" light I captured during my investigation of Berkeley is still unexplained.

reflecting light from by camera – if I had used a flash. Instead, I had adjusted my camera to its highest light sensitivity setting and turned off the flash so not to blind the many investigators on the grounds with me. The only conclusion I'm able to draw from my knowledge of photography and my consultations with photo experts is that the "subject" of the image is something paranormal.

I was pleased with the collection of anomalous data that LeeAnne and I had put together. We were able to make that collection even better with suspect photos and audio recordings submitted to us by the other investigators who toured that night. One of those investigators, Jackie, passed along an audio recording made during a session of questions in the basement room where Berkeley employees had reported the feeling of being watched. Present during the recording were Jackie and two other women, but the voice that mysteriously imprinted itself onto her tape was definitely male. Jackie goes through several questions and then asks, "Can you say it again please?" In a clear, easily understood response, the man says, "I told him they could call."

We were all puzzled by his statement yet exhilarated from the clarity of the message. Who was this man and who would he need to tell about our visit? The latter question and its possible answers sent chills up my spine, but nothing that would compare to the Electronic Voice Phenomenon I received from Herman.

Herman is a professional firefighter with sharp attention to detail. He is a great investigator to work with because of his grace under pressure, surely a carryover from his job, and his ability to find minute anomalies in audio, video, and photographic data. Not wanting to miss anything of importance, Herman filmed our entire tour with a digital video recorder. He caught our most astonishing piece of data from the night, a tiny voice nearly lost in another conversation, while reviewing the footage for traces of the paranormal.

When I heard Herman's recording for the first time, I was at a complete loss for words. Photos I had taken in the graveyard at Berkeley spun through my head. Why did I suddenly have the strange feeling of déjà vu? I tried to pin it down, but the only thing I was able to do for several minutes was repeat the audio clip.

I brought together dozens of investigators who had attended our tour at Berkeley to hear and discuss this remarkable capture – and all were astonished with the findings.

The DVR recorded a member of our group asking Sue, the tour guide, a question about one of the Harrison men. As Sue paused to think of her answer, the voice of a young child chimes in and says, "My name is Lottie." Lottie was the daughter of William A. Harrison, the daughter who died at only ten years old and was buried in Berkeley's cemetery. There was no mistaking her message – she was there and she wanted us to acknowledge her.

LeeAnne and I returned to Berkeley a few weeks after our initial visit to present the findings the group had collected. All of the staff stayed late to see what we discovered, and I think some were surprised that we had so much to share.

We watched a slide show of dozens of images of orbs and then shared my unnerving photo of the "angelic" light anomaly. Next we explained the two scent-related phenomena of the evening and discussed the mysterious shutoff of the two video cameras. The grand finales of the presentation were our prize audio recordings from the investigation

– two "Class A" Electronic Voice Phenomena. We had everyone don headphones to hear the voices individually and try and distinguish, with no guidance from LeeAnne or myself, what the messages conveyed. The looks of shock and fascination on the staff's faces spoke volumes. Any doubts they had about a paranormal presence at Berkeley were cast aside with the sound of Lottie's brief announcement.

I'm not sure if it was due to curiosity or excitement, but the plantation's tour guides asked if we'd be willing to leave some equipment running overnight in an attempt to capture more revealing data. It was difficult to hold back my first instinct to shout, "Of course!" but I managed to pull it off with grace. Never leaving home without *some* kind of investigative gear, LeeAnne and I retrieved a video camera and three digital audio recorders from the car and joined Michelin at the side door.

"Other than the areas we've heard stories about, is there anywhere else in the house you'd recommend we examine?" I asked.

With a moment of hesitation, Michelin answered in a hushed voice, "The third floor. Grace *never* let anyone up there, not even the exterminators when they were here to fumigate for bees. She told one of the former employees here that she'd heard a baby crying in there before.

LeeAnne and I exchanged nervous glances and followed Michelin into the house and upstairs. Michelin unlocked the Jamieson's private quarters and held the door for us to enter. The feeling that I was intruding again came over me as soon as I crossed the threshold. We climbed a steep staircase to a door on the ceiling. The door looked just like all the others in the living quarters, but its strange placement made me wonder if I'd just stepped through the looking glass.

I helped Michelin push up the door until the counterweight on the other side held it safely in place. The third floor, filled with odd antiques and boxes, was the size of my entire house. We prepared our recording equipment and stowed devices in three of the four bedrooms, and placed another in the large central hall from which all the rooms branched. I announced to the emptiness that if anyone was there and willing to communicate, they could speak to one of the machines and I may be able to receive their message later.

We tiptoed back through the opening in the floor and down the stairs, carefully pulling the door closed behind us. Taking a cue from my last visit to the Jamieson's quarters with Sue, I thanked Grace as Michelin locked up.

LeeAnne and Sue met us in the main hall on the first floor to discuss our plan for retrieving the equipment the following morning.

Lottie Harrison's grave.

Our four recorders would capture a total of thirty-two hours of data – the thought of what we might discover in that amount of time was exhilarating. The conversation shifted to the employees' reactions to the findings we'd presented earlier that evening. "I have something we could use to try and talk with Lottie right now," LeeAnne announced. She pulled a small black and silver box from her gear bag and explained that it was called the Ovilus I. The contraption was the creation of radical thinker and paranormal researcher, Bill Chappell. According to Bill, the Ovilus could enable spirits to communicate in real time by using tiny electromagnetic fluctuations that were then translated into words and phonetic sounds.

We were intrigued and all eagerly agreed to listen to what the Ovilus had to say. LeeAnne plugged in a set of portable speakers and switched on the device. A voice erupted from the machine almost immediately. It took us all a moment to get used to the monotone messages, but they became easier to understand the more we heard. The Ovilus was saying several words repeatedly: remember, hide, and wounds. None of those really proved that a spirit was trying to talk to us, but each word was increasingly unsettling.

The voice quieted after just a few minutes and we decided to ask a few questions to try and solicit a response. With silly images of old horror movies popping into my mind, I asked if there was a spirit present that would like to communicate. The voice crackled out of the speaker almost immediately. Its answer was, "Aye."

"Are you a member of the Harrison family?" Sue asked, likely hoping to get a response from Lottie. We waited for what felt like forever, but there was no reply. "Were you with General McClellan?" Another stretch of silence.

LeeAnne was next and asked, "Are you a child?" Again, nothing. I was beginning to feel a little discouraged. "Are you a man?"

"Aye," the voice replied.

"Are you a soldier?" I asked. Another positive response followed. I felt bold and wondered if the Ovilus and the spirit supposedly using it to communicate would answer more specifically. "What is your name?"

"Jack." We'd struck gold. The voice who claimed to be Jack had a lot to talk about. He kept going back to "wounds" and began giving cryptic messages about a "traitor." Benedict Arnold and his nasty surprise visit to Berkeley over 200 years earlier came to mind. Jack seemed to drift away after a while and the silence between his responses became longer and longer.

We moved to the south end of the hall and were only a few feet away from the dining room door when words suddenly sprang from

The main hall of Berkeley where we communicated with a spirit named "Jack." LOC Call Number: HABS VA, 19-CHARC.V, 4-22.

the Ovilus again. The first, and most disturbing, was "daddy." I looked at the three other women and watched their faces drain of color. I'm certain that mine was doing the same.

More words: sit, happy, talk, smile. The eager voice repeated "sit" over and over, until Sue finally asked, "Do you want me to sit?"

"Yes," the voice answered.

Sue took a seat on the antique velvet loveseat by the dining room door. The Ovilus demanded, "Talk. Happy, talk." We then watched as a small, round depression emerged on the seat beside Sue. She jumped, obviously startled by the movement so close by, and gave us a did-you-see-that look. Our wide eyes told her we did.

The questioning continued and the responses were mostly upbeat and pleasant. It seemed as though the spirit we were talking with was just eager for company and conversation. Eventually, either its energy weakened to the point it was no longer able to operate the Ovilus, or it just ran out of things to talk about. The silence returned.

We went outside to say our goodbyes and head for the parking lot when Jack announced he had more to say. Sue led the questioning and interpreted that Jack was hoping for some kind of help. None of us ever really felt qualified to help a spirit "cross over," or whatever it hoped to do. Thinking on her feet, Sue quickly asked, "Would you like us to say a prayer for you?"

"Aye," the voice said.

Sue and Michelin recited the Lord's Prayer, and when they finished, Sue asked the spirit if that was okay. The response from the Ovilus immediately lifted the solemn mood and had us all stifling giggles. "Check," it said.

I met Michelin the following morning and retrieved the equipment from the third floor. LeeAnne and I reviewed the recordings, an effort that took nearly two weeks, and discovered that all of the devices had captured the same unusual sounds in the empty attic. In no sort of pattern, we heard peculiar thumps, like objects falling or being dropped onto the floor. Each of the thumps was followed by an echo that led us to believe the noises were coming from in the room, not from inside the walls or from the typical sounds of a settling structure. One thump was so loud and close to a recorder that we could actually hear the device vibrate with the impact. In eight hours duration, the audio recorders captured over thirty of these sounds whose source is still unidentified.

The remarkable anomalies that we captured at Berkeley were enough to convince the experienced investigators present during our original visit that there were several spirits residing there. The staff of the plantation agrees. Their firsthand encounters on the grounds and in the mansion support the theory of multiple entities that run the gamut from calm and comfortable to grumpy and restless. Tourists of Berkeley continue to report what they believe are supernatural occurrences there, and the guides welcome their stories. Visit the plantation and you just might leave with a tale of your own.

⋙ *Westover* ⋘

estover Plantation, neighbor of Berkeley, lies on the bank of the James River at the end of a two-mile driveway lined with ancient cedars. The enormous brick house is considered one of the finest examples of Georgian architecture in the United States. Its stately presence is thanks to an equally impressive figure in Virginia history, William Byrd II, the founder of Richmond. As a display of friendship, and possibly to help strengthen political ties, Byrd named his estate in honor of Henry West, the son of then Virginia Governor Thomas West.

Westover, built around 1730, is the cornerstone of the elite class of mid-eighteenth century plantations still standing along the James. The home is a rare gem among Virginia plantations in that it still sits among the majority of its early workhouses and dependencies including an icehouse, well house, and kitchen. Except for the cars

Nearly all of the two-mile driveway to Westover is lined by giant cedars and working farmland.

parked in the nearby lot, Westover appears nearly the same as it did over a century ago.

The plantation has been so well preserved thanks to continual residency – it never sat abandoned like so many huge estates after the emancipation of slaves. Westover did, however, see a fair amount of turmoil during those Civil War years. McClellan's troops, encamped at neighboring Berkeley, spilled over onto the Westover grounds and left a wake of destruction on the land. The manor house itself even lost its famous Byrd Library, a collection of more than 4,000 volumes, to a fire in the East Wing during this period. The East Wing was rebuilt in 1900, and it and the West Wing were then connected to the main house.

Westover's long history of strength and perseverance may have spilled over to the home's residents – both in life and the beyond. The most famous ghost of Westover is Byrd's lovely daughter, Evelyn. Legend tells that Evelyn died of a broken heart after her father

forbade her to marry her Catholic love. She shut herself away from her family and lived alone in a small cottage on the Westover grounds. It was there she died in 1737.

Evelyn's good friend, Ann Harrison of Berkeley, is the first to claim to have seen her ghost walking near her grave in the cemetery at Westover Parish. Over the years, guests at Westover have reported seeing a young woman in eighteenth-century clothing strolling in the garden. The current lady of the house, Mrs. Fisher, told me during my visit that she and her children have often

A portrait of Evelyn Byrd graces the mantel in the rebuilt library of Westover's east wing.

caught glimpses of "someone" passing through doorways and around corners. She said the most unsettling thing about the experiences is that they're almost always accompanied by a chill in the air and a "swishing" sound, like the rustle of taffeta.

My personal interest in Westover plantation goes all the way back my childhood. I had the good fortune of growing up only three doors down from Mrs. Bruce Crane Fisher, former owner and manager of the historic estate. Mrs. Fisher moved to the quiet suburb on the edge of Richmond in the mid-1970s to enjoy a peaceful

retirement. The care and management of Westover were then passed to her son and daughter-in-law.

Mrs. Fisher was a kindhearted woman who loved to share stories with the neighborhood children. One talk she shared with me concerned the spirit of William Byrd III, whom she and her father suspected of haunting an upper bedroom at Westover. Byrd allegedly died of suicide in the house after an intense stretch of financial difficulty. Mrs. Fisher said that she always had an "uneasy" feeling in that room, but never saw or heard anything that she felt would cause harm.

The 250 years of ghostly lore at Westover gave me great hope of capturing some kind of evidence to support those legends. I journeyed to Charles City County at the peak of Spring's floral showcase. Wild roses peeked out from the woods that bordered the entry to the plantation's driveway. The driveway seemed to follow the same route it had for two hundred years, and in some places was nearly four feet lower than the surrounding farmland. I could hardly imagine how many carriages, horses, and eventually automobiles had taken this narrow road to the old Byrd estate.

I parked in the small grassy plot near the caretaker's house set up for that purpose and made my way through the brick pillars on either side of the walk to Westover's river entrance. On the other side of the gate, I was met by ancient tulip poplars and boxwoods. Some of the poplar trunks were at least eight feet across, but somehow they were perfectly proportioned to the grand brick manor.

I surveyed the grounds and wandered to the north side of the house, opposite the James River. The outbuildings of Westover formed a tiny village of sorts. The kitchen and laundry building was a sturdy stone and brick cottage that could have easily made

Westover Plantation today, after the connection of the east and west wings to the main house.

a cozy house. I assumed there was a lot of cooking and washing to be done when the building was constructed – it was the only way I could justify its size. I stepped though the door and found myself staring into a massive fireplace, so large that I could almost walk into it. There were giant iron kettles with paddles for stirring linens. Housekeeping and cooking implements from the eighteenth and nineteenth centuries lined the shelves on the end walls. It seemed as though the work had never stopped here.

The kitchen had a welcoming feel that made me somewhat suspicious. What was it about this building that was set aside for hard work that I found comfort in? Its intimate size and rough, earthy construction? I began to wonder if perhaps there was some kind of spirit presence there that was comforted by a female visitor. My imagination began shooting sparks in all directions, but I managed to get it under control and instead focused my energy on collecting photos and audio data.

I tucked my audio recorder into one of the iron cauldrons and concealed it with a giant spoon. I snapped about thirty photos before announcing that I was leaving for a short time. On my way out I added that I'd be happy to hear any messages that might be left for me on

An enormous fireplace is the focal point of the kitchen and laundry building.

The ice house is quite unusual from the outside.

the device in the pot. I figured it wouldn't hurt to make it clear that I wanted mutual communication.

The grounds were deserted except for two horses in a nearby field and a woodpecker ridding one of the giant tulip trees of a few pests. I ventured toward a peculiar little building at the east side of the manor house that, at first glance, appeared to have walls only about a foot high. Its steeply pitched roof only added to my curiosity. A plaque beside the door informed me that this was Westover's icehouse.

I opened the door with some reserve, not knowing what to expect on the other side (bats perhaps?) but found only darkness. I could make out the thin white line of a pull-cord, so I gave it a tug. The tiny building suddenly tripled in size – at the center was a deep brick chamber, about six feet across, that dropped about twenty feet into the cool clay earth. Above the opening hung an ancient ice tong. I peered over the wooden railing and took several photos of what was undoubtedly the largest and oldest refrigerator I'd ever seen. The same feeling of calm and welcome hung in the ice house that I sensed in the kitchen. Normally, being alone in a dark and creepy little building like this one would have had me on edge, but I found only the opposite. I was eager to leave the audio recorder here for a while after it had completed its mission in the kitchen.

I switched off the icehouse lamp and squinted as I climbed out into the sunlight. My third stop was right next door – the well building. I was met again by darkness and a faint white pull cord. Instead of

This massive brick-lined pit would have held enough ice to help preserve food through Virginia's warm seasons.

illuminating the inside of the building, the lights in the well house were tucked below ground level and lit the interior of the well shaft. It dropped further into the earth than the shaft in the icehouse, but this opening was much narrower. I could make out what appeared to be a "T" intersection at the bottom of the well shaft where it and a horizontal tunnel met. I remembered this tunnel from the legends associated with Westover. Locals believed that the tunnel connected to the manor house at one end and opened to the river at the other, allowing the family and servants opportunity to flee Indian attacks. The legend was recently laid to rest when archeologists determined that the tunnels were really only a primitive form of air conditioning. Convection currents created by the slope of the shafts pulled cool air into the mansion to provide some relief from Virginia's harsh summer heat. Still, looking down that well shaft to the connecting tunnel below brought a chill that raised the hairs on my neck.

After moving my audio recorder from the kitchen to the icehouse, I continued to explore the estate. My next stop was the immaculate formal garden. Shaded paths and flowering shrubs taller than six feet cleverly concealed several turns. A breeze rustled the canopy overhead and brought an eerie sensation that I was not alone.

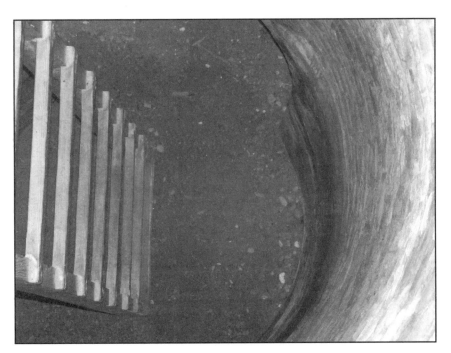

A look down the well shaft offers a glimpse of the connecting tunnel at the bottom.

I took my time in the garden and was careful to note any change in my surroundings. I photographed every corner, and turned to discover the grave of William Byrd II only a few yards in front of me on the path. The monument atop it looked weathered and beaten, but was still elegant. A cool breeze spilled from a path of peonies and wound around my ankles. Was someone or something trying to get my attention? I waited a bit, snapped more photos, and headed back to the icehouse without incident.

I moved my audio recorder to a third location, the dry well, and left it to capture whatever sounds may present themselves. I took a stroll and met the horses, photographed more enormous trees, and admired Byrd's grand iron gates. The only noise on Westover's grounds was a light breeze and the occasional call of an eagle over the river. Everything in the setting evoked serenity.

About ten minutes after placing the recorder in the well house, I retrieved it and left for home to comb through the data I had collected.

Several days of photo analysis turned up nothing out of the ordinary. Every image seemed to be pulled from a postcard and made me feel welcome. The audio recordings, on the other hand,

Lush foliage concealed several turns in the garden.

offered two peculiarities that left me feeling a little uneasy. In one track, I heard myself placing the recorder in the iron kettle in the kitchen building, snapping photos, saying a few words to any spirits that might be present, and then leaving the structure. Only a few seconds later, the recording ended – it had somehow been physically stopped. The batteries were strong and lived through more than an hour of recording beyond that point, so I ruled out a power failure. There had been nothing in the kettle except for the giant wooden spoon. It had concealed the recorder but never touched it. I was at a loss for a natural explanation.

The second recording that caught me by surprise was captured in the well house. The audio device was recording the sounds of the "empty" building when a sigh interrupted. The breath seemed to be light and feminine and sounded very close to the microphone.

Listening to the track sent chills through me. Could this have been Evelyn Byrd? She was the only female spirit thought to roam Westover, but she had only been seen and not heard. The Fisher family had reported the sounds of rustling fabric, but never anything similar to this sigh. Had I captured a sound of the past? I think anything is possible, especially at Westover Plantation.

The monument to William Byrd II.

✥ Kittiewan ✥

The James River and Kittiewan Creek meet on the edge of rolling green farmland aptly named Kittiewan Plantation. The modest eighteenth-century middle-class home sits at a hilltop, dressed informally in simple white clapboard siding. Compared to the grand estates commonly found in Charles City, Kittiewan seemed almost tiny. During my visit to the plantation, I discovered that the house felt more like a home than any of its historic neighbors. Perhaps that's the reason some of its former residents have yet to leave.

Kittiewan's roots run nearly as deep as the European settlement of Virginia. While the origin of the plantation is murky primarily because of its age, historians have been able to trace a land grant of the property as early as 1618. The home that stands as the centerpiece of the estate was first mentioned when Dr. William Rickman, a prominent physician during the Revolutionary War, purchased the plantation (then called Millford) in the early 1770s. Though a specific construction date has yet to be found, architectural dating of the brick foundation and chimney of the structure suggests that it was erected sometime before 1725.

Kittiewan Plantation feels like a warm and welcoming family home.

Dr. Rickman lived at Kittiewan with his wife, Elizabeth Harrison, of nearby Berkeley Plantation, until his death in 1783. The property changed hands several times within the Harrison family and was host to many tenant farmers until 1846, when it was sold to another physician named Dr. William Selden.

The Selden family was quite large and it is thought that the majority of the changes to the farmhouse were made during their residency in order to accommodate their many children. Dr. Selden set up his practice in a small building on the grounds and he and his family thrived at Kittiewan until the Civil War drove them out in 1863.

The plantation was again thrust into a decades-long pattern of buy, sell, and rent. It wasn't until 1912 that things finally settled down for the old farm when it was purchased by Loren and Nellie Clark of Michigan. The Clark's daughter, Wilma, grew up at Kittiewan and eventually married and brought her husband, William Cropper, to live there in 1948. In 2005, upon Mr. Cropper's passing, the estate was entrusted by the family to the Archeological Society of Virginia to assure its continued preservation and to provide an educational research facility for the Society and the public.

Thanks to the care of the ASVA, Kittiewan has been undergoing restoration in the years since Mr. Cropper's transfer of the site to the Society. A combination visitor center and archaeology lab has been built across the old country road from the original plantation house to welcome travelers and students.

I had an opportunity to visit Kittiewan a few weeks before they opened to the public in May, 2008. Rumors of paranormal activity swirled around the place, but none more specific than "strange things" that were known to happen in the home and on the grounds. My hope was to find out exactly what those strange things might be.

The weather was crisp and clear and I'd hoped to explore the grounds and capture some photos of the home's exterior against the bright blue sky. The long gravel road that led from the state highway to the farm at the riverfront was lined with cedars and surrounded by fields that had remained relatively unchanged for the past 200 years. Strangely, when I pulled up in front of the empty plantation house, I felt very welcome.

I had expected to find the site closed when I made the trip. I was pleasantly surprised to meet Tom, the no-nonsense repairman, at the driveway where he was installing a new sign in preparation for Kittiewan's grand unveiling. He pointed me towards Shirley, who was up to her shoulders in the home's ancient azaleas while clearing out weeds and underbrush, to take me on a walk through the house. It was a

Preparations were being made for the site's grand opening when I arrived.

workday, but both were friendly, hospitable, and obviously very pleased to share the plantation's progress with an unexpected visitor.

Shirley guided me through the first floor of Kittiewan and carefully explained what restoration the house had been subject to. The dining room table was set beautifully in high nineteenth-century style, but was strangely surrounded by glass display cases against every foot of wall, each case filled to the bursting point with antique cast iron toys. That's when I learned that Mr. Cropper had a deep passion for collecting – everything. The dishes that dressed the table were even part of one of his collections.

"The Archeological Society inherited at least eleven outbuildings completely packed with Americana when we took over care of Kittiewan," Shirley explained. "Mr. Cropper wanted to share his treasures with the public. We're trying to make that happen for him by rotating the displays in this room."

We moved to the music room in the southwest corner of the house. More of Mr. Cropper's carefully selected artifacts, like original Victrola Phonographs, Edison Cylinder Players, and an odd assortment of stringed instruments, set the mood. Two large nooks on either side of the fireplace were lined with books and old 78-speed records. The music room truly felt as though someone had simply stopped time in the early twentieth century.

After exploring the antiques in the music room for a while, and even helping Shirley crank up one of the old phonographs, we headed to the home's famous "Panel Room" in the southeast corner.

I was awestruck by the architectural detail that seemed to decorate every inch of the space. Century-old gray milk paint gave a spooky feel to the arch-topped paneling that lined the walls. Tiny dental molding hung in neat rows near the high ceiling. Ripples in the ancient glass windowpanes reminded me for a moment of the soft waves on the James River just a short distance on the other side of them. Though I saw no one, the uneasy feeling of someone joining us in the room then became difficult to ignore.

Shirley gave me a little more insight on the chill that had started to creep up my spine when she said, "We think this

The Panel Room houses more of Mr. Cropper's collections, and perhaps the spirit of the man himself.

part of the house is the oldest. Also, in the last years of his life, Mr. Cropper moved his bedroom in here because he liked the light. I think he also felt better being on the ground floor." I was wondering if he was still around the old Panel Room enjoying its relaxing morning light when I heard the back door open and close at the end of the hall. "Oh, here's Patrick, our historian!"

Patrick answered a few of the questions I had about the site and informed me that an archeology field school was about to conduct a dig the following week in an attempt to locate the foundations of some of the farm's former outbuildings and the site of the early gardens. Though Kittiewan is still considered a working farm, its focus in the early twenty-first century is certainly different than it was 200 years ago. Instead of planting and harvesting grains and tobacco, the work on the plantation today revolves around finding clues to daily life of the middle class in early Virginia.

Patrick excused himself and went to work repairing some trim in the Panel Room while Shirley and I climbed the stairs to view the old bedrooms on the second floor. The low, angled ceilings upstairs were in stark contrast to their high counterparts below. All of the upper rooms felt welcoming and cozy. We walked through the Green Room while Shirley told the back story of the furnishings, linens, and clothing on display that had belonged to Wilma Cropper's family, the Clarks. Through a narrow door that had once been a dormer window opening, I found another small room decorated and furnished as a child's playroom from the late nineteenth century, complete with spooky toy cradles and dolls. The feeling of being watched overcame me again and I made a quiet comment about the room having a strange vibe.

"There's probably a good reason for that," Shirley said. "We think that there's a ghost of a little girl still here. She's probably one of the Rickman's or Selden's daughters, but we're not certain. Tom's heard her several times," Shirley explained. "The first time he heard her, it spooked him pretty good, but he's getting used to it."

Curiosity was killing me. I had dozens of questions spinning in my head, but only managed to muster, "What does she say?"

"He says that he's only heard her say, 'Daddy?' like she's looking for someone. The last time he heard her ask, he said 'I'm in the kitchen,' but didn't

Soft orbs appeared in photos taken in the Green Room.

get a reply. Tom said she's been quiet for a while but he has a hunch she'll be back."

"Has anyone else heard her?" I asked.

"Not that they'll admit. Some of the folks that helped with the work on the house are quick to change the subject when you bring it up," Shirley replied. "Pretty much everyone agrees that they've had the feeling that there was someone else around when they were working in a room alone, though."

Maybe the little girl was the cause of the "strange things" that were rumored to occur in and around the house? I couldn't help but wonder why exactly she was calling for her father. I also wondered if she was the only spirit still roaming the old house. With so many antiques in the building, how could anyone really be sure that she was tied to the house itself and not something else there? The situation was very sad but intriguing at the same time.

We wrapped up the house tour in what was set up as the "masculine" bedroom at the western half of the upstairs. Shirley graciously allowed me to take more photos of Kittiewan's interior before we moved outside. She beamed like a proud parent at my fascination with the home the entire time I was snapping away with my camera.

My exploration of the plantation's exterior revealed a strange little red door on the building's west wall – it appeared remarkably well built for a simple cellar hatch. My observations were right on. Shirley informed me that the door was actually another one of Mr. Cropper's odd collectables and that it had once been the door to the old Charles City jailhouse. That certainly explained its heavy-duty structure. "Mr. Cropper bought the door to save it from the landfill when they tore down the old jail. He needed a place to display it, so he decided to dig out the crawl space and make it into an actual basement in the early 1980s," she said. Now *that's* a dedicated collector.

After roaming the grounds and collecting nearly all of the photos my camera could hold, I bid Kittiewan farewell. My visit was truly a pleasure, but it was all work when I returned home to examine the photographs and the audio recording I made of Shirley's informative tour through the historic home. I hoped that the recording would provide more than just details of the plantation's past – I was looking for Electronic Voice Phenomena.

All of my photos from the exterior and the first floor of the house looked more like shots from an upscale real estate

A door once belonging to the Charles City County Jail now serves as an entrance to the basement.

listing than a ghost-hunt. The images of second floor, however, provided more than just interesting architectural details. Several photographs in the "Green Room" contained unexplained blurs and points of light around the antique dresses that belonged to the women of the Clark family. Sadly, my audio recording contained nothing unusual that I could say offered support to the photos, but Shirley's story about the activity on the second floor was enough to keep the data from being written off as a fluke.

Kittiewan's cozy atmosphere is remarkably different from the other more "grand" plantations along the James River. The warm and eclectic lived-in feeling there encourages one to stay a while. Perhaps the young spirit that is believed to inhabit the old home is eager to entertain visitors?

❧ Piney Grove ❧

To describe in detail the wonders at the historic Southall Plantation is to try and tell 200 years of American history in only a few pages. Instead, I'll share with you the story of how a handful of buildings (and their ghosts) came together on a historic site in Charles City County. The grounds, once inhabited by Algonquian Indians, are now home to two plantation houses, a house containing a rare example of early Tidewater log architecture, a church relocated from North Carolina, a small cemetery, and several spirits whose origins are uncertain.

Furneau Southall, former deputy sheriff of Charles City County, established his lavish plantation at a bend in Glebe Road, between the James and Chickahominy Rivers, in 1790. Southall was a very influential man who worked closely with Benjamin Harrison of Berkeley, Ottoway Byrd, son of William Byrd III of Westover, and John Tyler. All that remains of his estate today is the former corn crib, which has evolved over the centuries and is now incorporated into the eastern portion of the building known as Piney Grove.

Piney Grove is the home of the Gordineer family. They painstakingly restored the structure over five years, from 1987 to 1992. Change and renewal have continued at the site long after the completion of their work to the historic building.

Brian Gordineer appears to have inherited his parents' love of preservation. He moved to Southall's Plantation with his wife, Cindy Rae, and brought a house known as "Ladysmith" there shortly after. Ladysmith began its life in Caroline County in 1857. It was the home of George and Maria Allen, who passed ownership down through their family, where it remained until 1974. The house sat empty and forgotten until 1987. Brian and Cindy Rae, after learning the home was to be demolished, purchased the building and had it carefully disassembled and moved to Charles City. The home has been beautifully reconstructed on its new site and even rests comfortably with several trees and shrubs from its former place in Caroline. The Gordineers furthered their honor of the structure's history by dedicating its suites to members of the Allen family. Ladysmith is now used as lodging for plantation guests.

Isabell, the youngest resident at Southall's Plantation at only ten years old, believes that a mischievous presence favors the Ladysmith

The Ladysmith House at Southall's Plantation.

house. She told me of several peculiar accounts of toilet lids and seats left up in the suite when no one was occupying the house. Isabell claimed that she and her mother would close all of the lids only to find them open again several days later. Brian added that many guests claimed that they felt they were not alone or had the strange sensation of being watched when they stayed in those suites.

Ladysmith and Piney Grove welcomed more company with the addition of Ashland and Duck Church in 1996. Though the two "new" buildings are physically connected, their backgrounds are very distant.

Ashland was originally constructed in 1835 in nearby James City County. The modest house was considered a "middle-class" plantation, similar to Kittiewan, and was the home of William H. and Susan Morecock. Ashland was believed to have been used as a schoolhouse in its past and was the property of a schoolteacher for several decades. The house was another of Brian and Cindy Rae's demolition rescues. They purchased Ashland and moved it to Southall's Plantation when they found it was to be leveled to make room for a golf course in 1994.

Brian learned of a murder supposedly committed in the house in the late nineteenth century. The story came to him from an elderly

Ashland was moved to the site from nearby James City County.

resident of James City who recalled the tale as it was passed to her. She claimed that the man killed at Ashland was shot in his sleep because he failed to settle his outstanding gambling debts. Brian and Cindy Rae investigated the master bedroom and found the bloodstained floorboards that supported the woman's story. Their attempts to identify the victim or the murderer in historical documents and James City County records, however, were fruitless.

Ashland's gloomy past seems brightened somehow by the addition of Duck Church at the rear of the house. Duck Church, the most unusual of all the adopted buildings at Southall's Plantation, was built around 1917 in Duck, North Carolina, for use as a schoolhouse. The structure was sold only a few years later to the local Methodist congregation. The attendance of the church, as well as the tiny town of Duck, grew until the church needed to be removed from the site to make room for a new building in 1990. Of course, Brian and Cindy Rae were quick to save this architectural and cultural jewel. They spent two years, 1994 to 1996, reassembling it and now use it as a spacious addition to their home at Ashland.

The Gordineer-Hart clan shares its passion for history and preservation with travelers and guests. The grounds are open daily, and the family operates an incredibly comfortable and hospitable bed and breakfast at Piney Grove. However, one of their specialties, an introduction to the spirits there, did not require an overnight stay.

Brian, Cindy Rae, and Isabell graciously hosted a private evening tour for me and a group of about twenty other investigators in the sticky June heat. Brian guided us and allowed us to snap photos wherever we pleased. He was also quick to answer our dozens of questions about the site's history. Ashland was the first stop on our tour.

The building was remarkably cozy, which seemed only fitting when I learned that it was the family's private residence. The comfortable touches, like the library with family photos lining the walls opposite the bookshelves, almost made me forget about the

Duck Church was added to the rear of Ashland to serve as a spacious bedroom.

mysterious murder that occurred there. The place was filled with antiques, each with its own well-documented past. For example, the rich, warm wood cabinetry and shelving in the kitchen were formerly parts of the Post Office at Cumberland Courthouse, Virginia. The downside to Ashland's unique blend of history, like that of nearby Kittiewan, is that it creates difficulty in determining if potential paranormal activity there is due to the building itself or some peculiar artifact inside.

We left Ashland and gathered in the yard for Brian to give us some bits of history about Duck Church. I was standing about eight feet from him when I noticed a strange distortion moving from right to left, towards Brian. The disturbance was like a blurry bubble, similar to the effect seen through a fisheye lens. My camera was still on from our walk through the house, so I quickly took a few photos where I'd seen the whatever-it-was.

I was trying to rationalize what I'd seen as my contact lens moving on my eye (though I'd never seen anything like it before in ten years.) What I saw on my camera's quick preview, though, didn't support my logical explanation at all. Near Brian was a round blur, about the size of a basketball, exactly where I thought I saw something with my

A strange "bubble" appeared to float towards Brian while he was explaining the history of Duck Church to his guests.

The high ceilings of Duck Church create a very different atmosphere from the rest of the buildings on the site.

own eyes. I bit my tongue to contain my excitement and went into a photo frenzy, shooting about a dozen more frames.

My mind was still spinning as we rounded Ashland and entered Duck Church. I was completely unprepared for the chill that hit me as I crossed the threshold – every hair on my arms and neck stood on end.

Inside the plain and simple church were gorgeous exposed beams that accented ceilings nearly twenty feet high. Every inch of every wall was decorated with antique portraits and religious items. It felt as though a hundred eyes turned to look at me at once. Resisting the urge to turn and leave, I managed to press my shutter button a few times. Using the excuse of wanting to make room for other investigators on the tour to enter, I moved back out to the garden to make some notes.

Brian came out just a few minutes later and I asked him if anyone had ever had an unusual or ghostly encounter in Duck Church. He told me that visitors have only remarked how charming and peaceful the building was. I agreed with the charming comment, but reserved my opinion about the spookiness that seemed to saturate the place.

Piney Grove was where the family's first ghostly encounter on the property occurred.

The rest of the group trickled out of the church and we crossed the grounds together towards Piney Grove, the oldest structure on the property. Brian knew that we were all there because of the rumor of ghosts, so he was eager to share a poem written by a family friend about the Gordineer's first supernatural experience at the plantation. The poem described Brian's father and brother working hard to repair structural pieces of the house in the basement below the old corn crib before the family moved in. They finished for the day and were on their way to nearby Williamsburg when his father noticed that he had left behind something very important to him – his watch. The two men returned to Piney Grove and began searching the basement for the watch. While they were looking, the thump-creak-thump of footsteps came from overhead. The men froze. The footsteps walked about three-quarters the length of the house and stopped. Brian's father and brother then tiptoed upstairs, fully expecting to catch a trespasser or vagrant planning on squatting overnight. They found no one in the house or in sight on the grounds. Brian said that his father later surmised that it must have been one of the deceased owners checking in on the work being done to his former home.

After reading the poem, Brian told us about architectural and archeological finds made in the basement where his father and brother had been working. Oyster shells and other signs of Native American life were discovered, as well as the signs of set wooden posts thought to have been part of a Native American structure on the site. The fertile fields and the nearby creek undoubtedly made the area a prime location for Virginia's early Algonquians.

We were escorted through Piney Grove's main entrance, into the dining room that separated the older portion of the house from its newer additions, and finally into the old log room that began life as a corn crib. The energy in the room was odd and seemed to buzz, like a television set had been left on with the volume down. No such TV existed, so I could only conclude the feeling came from *something* in there that I couldn't see, but from what, I didn't know.

We heard a story about how this section of the building had survived a fire in centuries past. Some of the exposed logs of the ceiling still showed scars and blackening from the blaze. Brian told us the older structure had been used as a store in the nineteenth century. This small area, probably only s600 square feet including

The log structure in the oldest portion of the Piney Grove house still shows faint century-old scars of smoke and fire.

the tiny room upstairs, had witnessed many monumental changes, both good and bad. It currently functions as a rustic breakfast room for B&B guests.

The group snapped several photos and shuffled outside. I made sure I was the last one out – that prickly energy still had my attention and I wanted to shoot a few more photographs. In all,

I captured about fifteen images in the quiet room. Half of them, each taken without flash, offered some surprising findings. Small, cloudy balls of light like orbs appeared near the ceiling. Never before had I seen so many anomalies caught in a sequence of photos without a flash. I thought that surely this was some kind of fluke, until the other investigators presented similar findings to me later.

I ran to catch up with the rest of the group and joined them at the tiny gate of the Harwood Family Cemetery. The little plot was surrounded by a beautiful iron fence that showed off the work of skilled Victorian craftsmen. Inside the graveyard was a dense mass of iris, their tall leaves nearly obscuring the only gravestone. Brian explained how the cemetery had been so overgrown when his family purchased the property that they didn't even realize it was there. When they found it, they cleared out the brush, leveled the soil where the graves had sunken, and reassembled the fence. Now it blended in like another lovely garden on the grounds. The Gordineers later learned from a visitor that the graves all belonged to young children. The eldest, Aubrey, was only twelve years old when he

Many lights and orbs appeared in photographs taken in the old corn crib. This one (near the ceiling) was captured without a flash.

The lonely grave marker of Aubrey Harwood.

drowned while fishing nearby. His is the cemetery's lone grave marker.

Like all paranormal investigators, my group loves an old cemetery. We each took dozens of photos, and a few left audio recorders in hopes of capturing spirit voices. Brian caught our attention when he announced that there were other graves on the property. We followed him to the woods edge near the ravine just south of Ashland.

"We found these graves by accident when we were building the shed. They're at the edge of the old fields and historians tell us they're most likely slaves," he said. A heavy sadness seemed to drift down on us while we looked upon the two long rectangular depressions in the forest floor. The woods felt like they were watching us closely, ready to swallow us if we made the slightest wrong move. I managed to take a few pictures and then moved out onto the open lawn a few yards away before the nagging sensation of unseen eyes baring down on me became more than I could stand.

Our tour concluded at twilight. We retrieved all of our stashed audio recorders and snapped a few more photos on the grounds before leaving. Everyone was eager to get home and review the data they collected, and it was only a few hours later that I began hearing about their results.

Several investigators shared images with tiny light anomalies. Most were captured in the log section of Piney Grove, but a few were from the adjacent dining room and in the B&B suites of the Ladysmith house. All were intriguing, but ultimately inconclusive. However, one piece of audio data picked up on a recorder left at the Harwood Cemetery had the group baffled. While we were in the woods visiting the slave graves, the audio recorder captured a few notes of a tune clearly whistled by a person. All of the investigators on our tour were together over an acre away from the cemetery and no one else was out walking the grounds. The source of the whistling was unknown.

The strange sensations I had in Duck Church and in the forest near the ravine were only my own observations – I had nothing physical to support them. The light anomalies present in photos taken by several investigators during our visit and my own images from the oldest part of Piney Grove led me to believe that maybe there really was something supernatural present at Southall's old plantation. The unknown whistler in the audio recording strengthened that opinion, but it was the strange "bubble" distortion I saw and the unusual photo I captured just seconds later that pushed me over the hump.

I've learned that people who live in haunted houses often grow so used to minor paranormal occurrences that they eventually don't even register them in conscious thought. Could that have happened to the Gordineers at Southall's Plantation? It's certainly a possibility. I am confident, though, that young Isabell, with her naturally inquisitive nature, and attentive visitors to the wonderful collection of historic buildings will not let any unusual activity slip by unnoticed. Perhaps one of them could be you.

❧ *Prestwould* ❧

he 1797 estate of the Baronet Sir Peyton Skipwith stands on a hilltop overlooking the Roanoke River in South-Central Virginia, only two miles north of the storybook town of Clarksville. The facts surrounding Sir Peyton's acquisition of the land are murky, but popular legend claims that he won the tract from William Byrd III in a marathon poker game. While Skipwith was rewarded with a very valuable site on which to build his manor house, it was losses like these that supposedly led to Byrd's suicide at Westover Plantation.

Construction of Prestwould was no easy undertaking. Local limestone was hauled for its foundation, brick manufactured on location, and its finishings shipped from England. In all, the massive seven-bay, three story home took over a decade to complete.

When Skipwith finally moved into his grand plantation, he came with his second wife (and former sister-in-law) Lady Jean. She had a well-earned reputation for having a strong and independent personality, which might explain why so many visitors to Prestwould and its staff believe she never left.

The wife of a plantation owner served as the business manager of the house, a far cry from the flowery Southern Belle of books and movies who has nothing to do but entertain guests and sip mint juleps. Lady Jean stepped up to her role as manager of Prestwould and became a homemaking mogul, sort of a Martha Stewart of her era. The plantation's financial records, household inventory, and garden plans are said to be the most meticulously kept in all of Virginia. In fact, when restoration experts from Colonial Williamsburg needed direction in outfitting a home or plotting a period garden, they referred to Lady Jean's Prestwould records as a guide.

Lady Jean Skipwith not only kept careful records of the business at the manor, she kept a watchful eye on those who worked for her. Clarksville residents today tell of her keen ability to estimate the amount of goods being transported to Prestwould by the level of the bateaus used to ship them. Lady Jean watched from her hilltop as low-riding boats came to dock and matched their deliveries to the amount she estimated them to carry. She

Prestwould Plantation in Mecklenburg County.

caught several shippers "skimming off the top" of Prestwould's supplies and had them punished. Her fierce reputation only grew.

After Sir Peyton's death in 1805, Lady Jean assumed full management of Prestwould – both the household details, of which she was already proficient, as well as the farm functions. Many believe she took on all of the responsibility because she didn't think anyone else could do a better job than her.

The Prestwould estate today is under the care of the Prestwould Foundation, a private organization established to restore and preserve the plantation and the artifacts associated with it. That doesn't seem to have stopped Lady Jean from keeping an eye on things, though. Staff and volunteers at Prestwould claim to hear footsteps throughout the otherwise unoccupied house at all times of the day and evening. Visitors frequently complain of "heaviness" in the house, and even report sensing a presence that seems to follow them from room to room.

One of the most compelling encounters reported at Prestwould was submitted by a preservationist working at the site. He said as he was unlocking the house one morning, he heard faint harpsichord music coming from some distant room. After standing in the open doorway for a few moments and scanning the grounds for a car that might indicate who had arrived before him, he stepped inside and called out "Hello." The music stopped immediately and the house fell silent. He found no one there.

The preservationist is not alone in his report. The residents of Clarksville claim that the mysterious music is commonly heard by landscapers and other workers on the plantation grounds.

Letters from Skipwith friends and associates from the late eighteenth century contain several compliments toward Lady Jean's musical talent. The ghostly harpsichord melodies are, without surprise, attributed to the lady of the house.

The spirit of Lady Skipwith is also thought to express her displeasure with certain aspects of her home's restoration by slamming doors – a frequent occurrence at Prestwould. Strangely, no one has ever seen a door slam. Volunteers report *hearing* the booming echo throughout the house only to discover a formerly open door closed upon inspection.

My visit to Prestwould was in early November, after the plantation had closed for the season. I went solely with the purpose of photographing the house and grounds, but held a bit of hope that I might experience *something* out of the ordinary there. The cool, dry air was crackling with static electricity, even so close to the river and nearby lake. The conditions for paranormal activity were good.

The long road to the manor was bordered by nearly a mile of ancient looking dry-stacked stone walls. The stones were more of the local limestone that I assumed was the same used in Prestwould's construction. They were mostly long and flat, but some seemed little larger than my hand. It must have taken years to build.

When I finally reached the great house, I was surprised to find a member of the Prestwould Foundation there wrapping up some end-of-season work. He welcomed me, told me which outbuildings were which, and went back to work while I set about photographing things.

The wind off of the Roanoke River moaned through the trees on the hillside. It added to the spooky ambience and made the grounds feel almost alive. While photographing outbuildings, the feeling of being watched from the main house was too much to ignore. I found myself looking over my shoulder every few minutes, but never saw anything out of the ordinary.

After scouring the estate and recording images of every stone and board, I headed back to the driveway where I found the man from the Foundation preparing to leave as well. I told him that I'd heard of Prestwould's ghost from the folks in town and wondered what he made of it all. With a twinkle in his eye, he replied, "I'm no authority on the supernatural, but I'll tell you for certain that many, many things go on here that I can't even *begin* to explain. None of it stands up to logic, so I figure the idea a ghost is to blame is the best presented so far."

While my photos from Prestwould did not reveal any specters, I couldn't shake the feeling I was not alone on the grounds. Maybe Lady Jean was watching to see if I was making a delivery that she would need to inventory? Perhaps she was merely suspicious of me, an unannounced caller, and wanted to make sure that I was there for the right reasons. Whatever the case, I understood better than ever why so many visitors to and employees of the plantation reported sensing a "presence" at Prestwould.

Sir Peyton's estate, or maybe more Lady Jean's, feels like it has a personality all its own. I encourage any paranormal enthusiast or history buff to visit this mesmerizing destination for a unique sampling of architecture and the unexplained. I've already planned my return trip for the start of the next season and, like the man from the Prestwould Foundation, I credit the ghost.

Stone walls, in some places crumbling and in others immaculate, border the driveway to the manor.

✻ Appomattox Manor ✺

*I*t had been nearly a year since my previous visit to the Eppes family plantation in the City Point neighborhood of Hopewell. Before, the weather had been clear and crisp with a wind blowing off the choppy water so icy it chilled me to the core. This time, it was the humidity that dominated while dark clouds rolled toward the manor from the west. The looming storm was exactly the thing I hoped would charge the atmosphere for paranormal activity.

Appomattox Manor was a family home for generations before the Civil War came to the grounds and changed its fate. The plantation is situated at the convergence of the James and Appomattox Rivers. Its strategic location made it a perfect base camp for the Union Army during the siege of Petersburg. Northern gun ships protected City Point day and night while shipments of supplies were sent from the wharf by rail to Union troops in battle nearby. The home of Dr. Richard Eppes became the Civil War equivalent of the Pentagon.

Through the period of Union occupation, from 1864 to 1865, Appomattox Manor was used as General Grant's headquarters, a supply station, and a field hospital for the thousands of men wounded in nearby engagements. Grisly scenes at the plantation during this time and the number of soldiers who perished on its grounds made the home a likely site for a haunting. Strangely, most of the paranormal activity at the Manor seems to involve the spirits of children.

My interviews while working on *Haunted Battlefields* uncovered a personal encounter reported by one of the maintenance staff at Appomattox named Sandy. One evening after finishing her shift and locking up, Sandy started down the walkway towards her car and suddenly felt the need to look back over her shoulder. When she did, she saw a young boy peering out of a second-story window. Sandy thought one of the neighborhood kids must have slipped inside while she was occupied, so she went back to the manor house to let him out. Her inspection turned up no one inside or out.

On this most recent visit to City Point, I talked with the ranger on duty, Erin, who had her own remarkable encounter to share. While guiding a tour through the first floor of the house, the only portion open to the public, Erin claims she became distracted by the sounds of what seemed like two or three children running and playing upstairs. She continued her tour and decided to remove the young pranksters when she was done. A few moments later, a woman in the tour group asked, "Do you hear that?" Since the noise was then obviously distracting visitors, Erin excused herself to go and investigate. Again, just like Sandy, Erin found no one else in the house. She said she would have been quick to dismiss it as her imagination if the guests in her tour group had not heard it, too.

The activity at Appomattox Manor during the time between my visits was not limited only to the sounds of ghostly children. Probably the most peculiar report came from the site's historical expert, Emmanuel. One afternoon while sweeping the porch at the home's east wing, Emmanuel claims he was surrounded suddenly by an intense, unmistakable odor of cigar smoke. He noted that there were no visitors on the grounds at the time. While trying to find a logical explanation for the aroma, he was overcome by the sensation of someone unseen standing nearby on the porch. Emmanuel knew that both Dr. Eppes and General Grant, whose cabin is in clear view from the east wing, were avid cigar smokers. He recalls expecting to see one of the men standing right behind him, but upon turning around, found nothing.

That's where I decided to start my investigation – the porch of the east wing. I hoped to capture some sort of photo or audio anomaly that would echo Emmanuel's experience and maybe give me some clue to the smoker's identity. I sat on the top step, switched on my audio recorder, and introduced myself to the emptiness. I asked if anyone present would care to talk with me and then waited silently for any response. A few hundred yards downhill, several vultures circled above Grant's cabin. I asked if there was anyone who could hear me, would they please shout their name into my voice recorder as loudly and clearly as they could manage. Again, I waited with anticipation. Finally, I asked if the person responsible for the cigar smoke that startled Emmanuel was present, and if so, did they have a message for him?

It is strange sometimes how I feel I'm completely alone when I begin an audio session, but feel there is someone listening intensely to my every word when I conclude. That brief recording made on the east porch was one of those times. When I stood to leave, I even felt the need to thank those present for their time and to formally excuse myself.

Before leaving the plantation, I took a thorough walk through the first level of the house and made certain to take all the photos I could. My previous visit ended with my camera failing mysteriously in the oldest section of the home, and I intended to capture as many as possible this time around.

Like before, I found myself strangely attracted to an old oval mirror in the home's parlor. It had an ornate gilded frame and just enough darkening to the reflective surface to create an eerie illusion of movement in the room. I photographed it and the rest of the parlor before moving to the library across the hall.

Dr. Eppes' Library was simple by today's standards, but clearly set him apart as a gentleman of intellect in his time. A tall book cabinet still protects many of the doctor's personal volumes, including a family Bible that accompanied him on his extensive travels. I figured that if the doctor was visiting the manor now and then, he'd certainly want to check in on his possessions. My hope was that I could capture

some sort of indication that Dr. Eppes was in the room. Since no one was around, I called out into the empty library, "Dr. Eppes? Could I please take a photograph of you?" After a few moments, I began snapping away with my camera. "Thank you. You have a lovely home and it has been a pleasure to visit," I said. My belief is that one should always treat the dead as one would the living – with respect.

I made a final sweep through the house and thanked Ranger Erin for her help. About twenty yards or so from the front of the manor, while on my way back to the distant parking lot, I had the nagging sensation I was being watched. Sandy's story came to mind, but I looked over my shoulder and saw no one. My eyes were drawn up to the second floor windows and my camera was quick to follow. Were the playful children of the house seeing me off? Perhaps Dr. Eppes was eager to see what this curious caller chose for transportation? Maybe the mystique of Appomattox Manor had me caught in a spell, causing my imagination to get the better of me? I hoped that a careful review of the data I had collected that day could answer those questions.

I began my analysis with the audio recording made on the east porch, the location where the park ranger reported the cigar smoke and the uneasy feeling he wasn't alone. Though I try to go through each piece of data with a neutral mindset, I couldn't help but feel hopeful. In the recording I could hear the river lapping the stones at the shore nearby. The occasional squawk of a buzzard overhead interrupted my questioning, but I could make out no voice conveying any answers.

Appomattox Manor has an unusual "U" shaped layout that opens towards the waterfront.

A look into Dr. Eppes' cozy little library.

Moving on to the photos from the trip, I discovered a few small blurs in shots taken in the east wing of the manor and a single tiny orb captured in Dr. Eppes' library just after I had asked permission to photograph him. Though nothing obviously paranormal presented itself in the images, the few mysteries I did find went without a logical explanation.

I couldn't shake the sensations I'd felt at Appomattox Manor during my visits. Every step I took, I felt closely examined by unseen eyes. Every conversation with a ranger or guest felt as though a third party was listening in. While I cannot say for certain that one or more spirits reside at the manor, the park employees, those who spend the greatest length of time at the site, all agree that there is *something* present that defies logic and raises the hairs on one's neck.

The tranquility of this historic site in the midst of a modern industrial city makes it an ideal destination for locals and travelers alike. Perhaps you, on a windless day, could catch the scent of a phantom's cigar or have the rhythm of the river carry a whisper to your ear. With ghostly encounters being reported now with eerie regularity, I know I'll be visiting more often.

≫ Weston Manor ≪

O nly a short distance upriver from Appomattox Manor in Hopewell is a striking Georgian plantation called Weston. The home was built in 1789 by William and Christian Eppes Gilliam. Christian, daughter of Richard Eppes of Appomattox, is said to have received the land as a wedding gift from her father several years before the manor house was erected.

Despite the years of turmoil during the Civil War and the destruction that surrounded Weston, the home has retained nearly all of its original woodwork and structural detail of the interior. I couldn't help but wonder what else, or who else, its walls may have preserved.

Before my visit to Weston Manor, I had the pleasure of reading the diary of Emma Wood. Emma was a young girl during those tumultuous war years and spent some time of refuge at the Manor

Weston Manor is a prime example elegant architectural symmetry.

after her family was forced to flee their home in Hampton. She described, with the sharp attention of a child, her daily life at Weston – including accounts of the noisy ghosts who often "ran rampant" in the house.

One tale of troublesome spirits in the home resulted in many sleepless nights for the family and an eventual alteration to the building. The door to the guest bedroom was said to rumble and shake violently for several nights in a row. One evening, the occupants of the room claimed the door made such a commotion that the basin and pitcher on the nearby washstand threatened to crash onto the floor. In a moment of sleep-deprived desperation, one of the men in the house removed the door from its frame, installed the hinges on the opposite side, and replaced the door. To the relief of generations of Weston residents, it has been quiet ever since.

I toured Weston on a damp and gray afternoon in early October. The weather added just the right dose of spookiness to the otherwise welcoming house.

The entryways to the manor are unusually large for the period in which it was constructed.

Rich colors adorn every wall in Weston. This room, the study, is a deep red.

The first thing that struck me as unusual about the home was its location. It was nestled comfortably between the bank of the Appomattox River and a charming suburb of 1920s Sears Catalog Homes. A thick screen of trees set Weston apart from its neighbors and allowed me to quickly dismiss the abrupt change in setting.

Another thing that caught my attention about the Manor was its huge doors. The entrances at both the river and roadside porches were unusually tall and wide. Instead of the typical six-panel doors, Weston's doors were made up of nine panels. I felt like a small child as I stepped through them.

The peculiarities I noted outside were swept to the back of my mind as soon as I entered the house. I was struck by the carefully preserved staircase with its delicate curve, the detailed doorframes, and the precisely cut dental moldings in the main hall. The sunny yellow walls were a drastic contrast to the gray skies outdoors and seemed to warm me as I passed between them. I felt completely at ease.

With my audio recorder running, I explored the gentleman's study, the parlor, and the dining room, complete with a working dumbwaiter. The Eppes family connected with Thomas Jefferson's through marriage, and Jefferson's influence was easy to see throughout the home.

I ventured to the second floor and found the nursery, children's room, guest room, and master bedroom. After carefully examining the doorway of the guest bedroom, I assumed that there must be at least some small root of truth to the legend I had heard – the hinges of the door had clearly been moved to the opposite side. I took several photos of the room and its door when I remembered an encounter told to me by a former member of Weston's cleaning staff. The cleaning woman said she'd been working on neatening the bed in the guest room when she felt a sudden and firm yank on her ponytail. The tug, forceful enough to pull her head backwards, startled her more than it frightened. Though she continued to work at Weston for a long time after the incident, she claims she never felt completely comfortable in that room again.

I was standing near the bed, admiring a mourning dress on a mannequin only a few feet away, when I felt a distinct tingle on my scalp. The cleaning woman's story crossed my mind, and

A close inspection proved that the restless door had been re-hung.

I waited for a pull on my hair, but none came. I took dozens more photos in the room and then moved across the hall to the master's quarters.

The bedroom was furnished very simply and contained only a massive four-post bed, armoire, and a chair positioned near the west window. Somehow, though, the room still managed to have a crowded, oppressive feeling. The tightness became more pronounced, so I collected another series of photos for my records and headed back downstairs.

My final stop at Weston was the basement. A guide fetched the keys and we entered though an exterior door on the east side of the house. The basement had thick, rough brick walls and a swept dirt floor. The ceiling was very low, but allowed a clear view of the beams and planks that gave the home its strength. This area had been used as a kitchen and laundry during winter when the heat it produced could radiate throughout the home. In the summer, work was moved to a separate building and only the final preparations of food and its cleanup remained in the basement.

The brick hearth was ample and it displayed many of Weston's original iron cookpots. Again, I clicked away with my camera for several minutes before the guide led me back outside. I switched off the audio recorder, tucked my camera in my bag, and made it to my car just as the sky turned loose heavy drops of cold rain.

I was eager to examine the photographs and sounds I had recorded that day in hopes of finding anything that could support the stories of unusual activity at Weston. If I did discover something, my greatest reward would be to uncover a clue to the identity of the disruptive phantom.

Of the two hundred photos I snapped, only two contained anomalies. These numbers were not bad, rather more of what I considered "average" for a site with the age and reported paranormal activity of Weston. The first anomaly was a large, milky white orb photographed above the four-post bed in the master bedroom. The shape was not recorded in the shots taken immediately before or after the suspect image, and all were taken under the same conditions only moments apart.

The second anomaly was an orb of similar size and appearance which was captured in my last photo of the day – a shot of the basement hearth. Reviewing the image gave me an eerie, almost embarrassed sensation that I had unknowingly interrupted important work in progress.

A single orb appeared over the bed in the master bedroom.

Another light was captured over the mantel in the basement kitchen.

I carefully examined my audio recording, nearly forty-five minutes in length, over the course of several days. Despite my best efforts to detect anything that might be considered paranormal, I heard only the sounds of my guide's voice and the whirring of my camera motor.

My brief investigation of Weston yielded promising results. Though I didn't uncover the identities of the mysterious hair-puller or door-shaker, I am optimistic that clues will eventually present themselves, perhaps to someone unsuspecting. I encourage all visitors to the Manor to bring a camera and gratefully accept the Historic Hopewell Foundation's allowance of photography throughout the home. You could very well leave with a special souvenir.

❧ *Eppington* ❧

I was truly unprepared for what I discovered on a hilltop near the banks of the Appomattox River in Chesterfield. The plantation established by Francis Eppes IV, appropriately named "Eppington," is one of the three Eppes family farms still standing along the river. This one though, is far different from its cousins. Unlike the restored Weston Manor and Appomattox Manor, Eppington stands as a true "diamond in the rough" and offers a unique, almost behind-the-scenes look at the daily lives of two historic Virginia families – and a spirit who is said to linger.

Francis Eppes attended the College of William & Mary and became good friends with Thomas Jefferson. The two eventually married sisters, Francis to Elizabeth Wayles and Thomas to Martha Wayles Skelton, turning their bonds of friendship into that of family. After Martha's death in 1782, Thomas entrusted his children to the care of Francis and his family while he served as Minister to France. It was during that period that tragedy stuck.

Lucy Elizabeth, Jefferson's youngest daughter, was taken ill with whooping cough. Though she was well cared for by her sister and the Eppes family, little Lucy could not fight off the disease. She passed away in 1785 at age three. There are conflicting historical accounts of Lucy's burial site – some state she is

Eppington's carriage entrance.

interred at Eppington, while others claim she rests at Jefferson's Monticello. No conflict, however, surrounds the belief that her spirit still remains at the Eppes estate in Chesterfield.

I was graciously allowed into Eppington, now only open to the public by appointment or on their annual "Eppington Heritage Day" in October, by a representative of Chesterfield County's Parks and Recreation Division. Bryan, my guide, warned me to watch my step as the site was "rough" and had been undergoing some structural studies that required holes to be made in unexpected places.

We entered through a back door into the portion of the manor house added in 1900. Tall, cavernous ceilings echoed the groans from the floorboards and amplified our voices like we were in an amphitheater. Fragments of wallpaper hung several feet above my head, topping expanses of brilliant yellow paint. Bryan explained that this had been the modern kitchen, and I had to remind myself upon noticing a massive cast iron stove that "modern" is a relative term.

He led me to the central portion of the house that dated from 1770. The ceilings stepped up another foot or two, or so it

The main hall doubled as the home's parlor.

Layers of history are clearly visible on the walls of the study.

Meals were cooked in a separate building, but this narrow passageway served as the "preparations room" for food before it was sent to the dining table.

The children's room and its adjacent hall make up the entirety of the third floor.

seemed, and our echoes grew even louder. I photographed the main hall, which I assumed doubled as the parlor, and we drifted towards the east side of the house. The next stop was a room that contained a display cabinet of artifacts that had belonged to Eppington's more recent residents – the Thweatt, Hines, and Cherry families. A tiny model of the manor house sat at the far end of the room and was dwarfed even further by the enormous buffet on which it sat.

The next twists and turns took us down a dark corridor, around a narrow staircase, and to Francis Eppes' study. There I noticed the evidence of the structural exploration Bryan mentioned – neat little holes had been made in different portions of the walls to determine what was behind them. An unusual, almost dovetail-like seam in several of the floorboards led me to believe that some interesting construction had occurred there at one point, and the exploratory studies certainly made sense. I'd never seen anything like it before.

In addition to the holes in the study, layers of wallpaper, paint, and plaster had been cut away from the room like rings of a tree. Bright cornflower blue paint covered the earliest layer of the wall and, with a little help from the morning sun, cast a brilliant glow in the room.

Next door to the study on the western end of the house was a small room with a door to the outside. Bryan told me that historians believed the narrow space had been used as a final preparation area for food brought in from the outdoor kitchen. After collecting photographs from this spooky little room, we backtracked to the tiny staircase and headed for the second floor.

There were two spacious bedrooms on the next level. The ceilings were much lower than those on the first floor, and the space felt more homelike as a result. A small walkway led toward the rear of the house, and a strange grouping of short staircases and a tiny landing connected it to the 1900 addition over the kitchen. "That door is locked and I don't have a key for it. I've never even been in there, so I don't know if it's unsafe, if a collection is being stored there, or what," Bryan said, pointing to the other side of the stairs. My imagination kicked into high gear. I love a house with secrets, and this place had several so far.

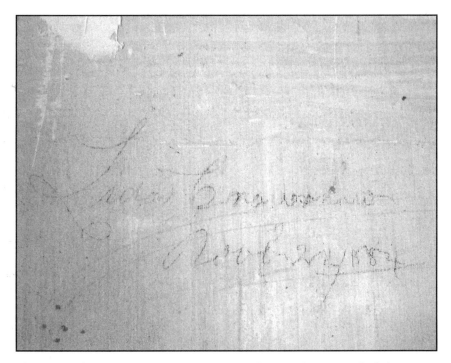

Signatures from many eras were uncovered upon the removal of the room's wallpaper.

"There's one more floor," Bryan added, "but the only room up there is the children's room." Bingo. That was exactly the place I had been hoping to see.

The last resident of Eppington, a descendent of the Cherry family, confided in a friend that she and her late husband had frequently heard the sounds of a small child in that room.

Sometimes the noises were only playful footsteps, but other times they were the heartbreaking sounds of inconsolable crying. She said that they always firmly believed it to be Lucy Jefferson.

Strangely, without any verbal exchange, Bryan stayed at the bottom of the stairs and waited for me to go exploring. I wondered if there was something I should know before going up, but resisted the urge to ask.

The stairs ended at a dark and wide corridor, wide enough to be considered a small room. A large bedroom lay off to the right and was bright and sunny in contrast to its neighbor. The walls, like many on the first floor, had been stripped of their former coverings and revealed all sorts of interesting scribbles. I could see where someone had been practicing writing the numbers eight and nine about two feet up from the baseboards. At eye level on another section of wall, I discovered several signatures, though none I could make out because the writing was so spidery and faded. One, however, was very clearly dated "1884." I was wondering what the person who penned that date wvould think if they knew someone was reading it over 120 years later, when I suddenly felt I was not alone.

Remnants of the schoolhouse at Eppington.

Only a few gravestones dot the spacious cemetery.

I stepped into a corner, faced out into the room, and began photographing the space. If there was a chance of capturing a sign of paranormal activity, I figured the uneasy feeling I had in the bottom of my stomach and on the back of my neck might be a sign that the odds were in my favor. I moved to the opposite corner and continued snapping images until the tingle in the air subsided. Reentering the dark corridor, I couldn't resist one more look back into the children's room. I thought I caught some movement out of the corner of my eye, but the room was empty.

Bryan and I wound our way back to the first floor, locked up, and ventured out into the yard. He showed me a crumbling old fireplace and chimney that were all that remained of the kitchen building. Downhill, closer to the river, sat a mass of stones that formed the ghostly footprint of a structure of some sort. "Historians and archaeologists think this was the schoolhouse,"

Bryan said. "All of the Eppes' children and Mr. Jefferson's likely attended, though we're not exactly sure of the age of the building." The cold, gray granite walls and the bare trees that stood between them made it hard to imagine it had ever been an inviting place to learn.

After answering more of my questions about the original and current uses of the property, Bryan and I headed back to our cars and drove a short distance down the driveway for a few photos of the family cemetery. He shared another disheartening bit of information with me before leaving: If Lucy Jefferson was buried there, there was no marker on her grave.

I finished collecting my photographs just as dark clouds floated across the sky and blocked out the sun. A strange sensation came over me as I got back in the car – it was as though someone or something was sad to see us go.

The Eppes estate has an atmosphere like no other plantation I've visited. The main house itself feels almost alive, like it's just waiting for some curious visitor (like me) to stop by so it can share a story or two. My stay there was brief, and I was correct in my suspicion that I had not captured proof of the paranormal in that short time. Do I believe that the last residents were imagining the events they experienced in the home? Absolutely not. I'm certain that some lucky tour group in the future will happen by at the right moment and they, like the Cherry family descendents, will have a special story to share about their time at Eppington.

❧ *Tuckahoe* ❧

An unusual H-shaped manor on the James River in Goochland County has been home to some of Virginia's most influential families since it was established in 1733. Rumor has it that some members of those families have yet to move on.

Tuckahoe Plantation, whose name comes from a Native American word for the edible plants that were once abundant in the area, was settled by Thomas Randolph in the early eighteenth century. Thomas' son, William, is credited with building the spacious home that still stands on the property today.

In 1745, William Randolph and his wife, Maria, passed away and left their four orphaned children in the care of William's good friend, Peter Jefferson. Peter and his family, including a toddler named Thomas, moved to Tuckahoe to assume responsibility of the Randolph farm and children. The Jeffersons lived at Tuckahoe from 1745 until 1752, when the eldest son of the Randolph's was able to take over the farm's operations at the ripe old age of twelve.

Today, the plantation serves as a fine example of the independence of eighteenth-century farms and the community that developed on the grounds of each. Tuckahoe boasts the most complete plantation layout in North America, with nearly all of its outbuildings intact on

Tuckahoe Plantation has an interesting "H" shaped floorplan.

its very own tiny main street. The estate still operates as a working farm and supplies local markets with a diverse selection of herbs and produce harvested from its hand-worked fields.

Aside from tourism and agriculture, Tuckahoe has a well-earned reputation as being *the* place to have an outdoor wedding. Its fairytale setting and gorgeous waterfront views make it a hard choice to trump. In addition to the fabulous wedding photos that couples take away from the plantation, some of luckier wedding parties leave with stories of their own encounters with the paranormal.

One local legend, made well-known statewide by ghost author L.B. Taylor in his *Ghosts of Richmond and Nearby Environs*, is that of a distraught spectral bride seen running down the garden path. Mixed claims of the bride's origins abound. One belief is that she is thought to have died of a broken heart after being left at the altar by her true love. Another popular explanation is that the woman was not jilted at all, rather her beaux was killed during the Civil War only days before his expected homecoming. After receiving the news, she allegedly waded into the river, wearing her wedding dress, and drowned. A third story of origin is that the young bride was forced to marry against her will and died from unhappiness.

Probably because of these stories, the crying bride is not a pleasant sight to see on one's wedding day and is thought to be a bad omen. If this ghost is more than a figment of the imagination, I feel she's likely only roused by the energy and excitement that surrounds the occasion. To see if I was on the right track, I set out for Goochland on the day before one couple's fall ceremony to try and coax the forlorn phantom out of hiding.

The October day was overcast and breezy. Gold and orange leaves fluttered down around me like confetti at a tickertape parade as I drove down the deserted River Road toward Tuckahoe. The spooky weather was perfect for exploring a haunted estate, and I hoped to make good use of it.

I turned onto the seemingly endless dirt driveway, passed by ancient fencing that was being swallowed by cedars planted too close to its posts, and caught the curious stares of sleepy-eyed black cows in neighboring field. I eventually made it to an empty parking area and unpacked my cameras.

The cedars at the end of the driveway closest to the house bent low over my head and let out numerous creaks and pops. I was beginning to entertain the idea that they were reaching down to snatch up an unsuspecting visitor when a jolly black Labrador Retriever ran to greet me. My new friend walked a step or two in front of me up the main walkway, turned to see if I was still following, and changed course – directly towards the famed Ghost Walk, the path on which the mysterious bride was often seen. I grew a little suspicious of the dog, but thanked her and gave her a scratch behind the ears anyway. She trotted off toward the outbuildings in the distance behind me.

In an open field just downhill from the Ghost Walk, I could make out the chairs arranged for the next day's wedding. I set up my tripod and started collecting images. The silence that blanketed the plantation was only interrupted by my shutter snapping. After about a half hour, the dog returned, only this time she brought company.

A brown-haired man with a rake in his hand waved hello and announced that his wife was the horticulturalist for the grounds. "Are you a wedding planner?" he asked. Not exactly, I thought. I told him I was there looking for the Crying Bride and hoped to take home a photograph of her. "There are plenty of ghosts here," he said. Plenty? I was intrigued and asked what he knew about the supposed spirits.

"Well, the Bakers, the family who lives here now, say they hear all sorts of strange sounds in the house. You know, footsteps, doors closing, whispering in another room, that sort of thing? One night they said they woke up to what sounded like a cocktail party going on downstairs – lots of people having a good time and talking. When they went to find out what was going on, the place was empty and locked up tight. They keep pretty quiet about it, though, maybe afraid it's bad for business or something." I had no reason to doubt that the family believed what they were experiencing was truly supernatural. Why else would they fear their observations might dampen Tuckahoe's reputation?

The Ghost Walk.

Thomas Jefferson's boyhood schoolhouse.

The man excused himself and headed downhill to a garden patch in need of tending. I returned to my camera and focused my attention to the house and the adjacent schoolroom. A weathered wooded plaque near the door of the tiny wooden schoolhouse indicated that it had been the place of Thomas Jefferson's earliest education. Since the building's footprint could have only been ten feet by ten feet at the most, I figured Jefferson had no choice but to be close to his books. After exploring and recording details of the house and grounds, I returned to the Ghost Walk for more photographs – just for good measure.

The farm as a whole had a very warm and welcoming air about it, much like the Retriever who met me at the driveway. There was nothing spooky or negative that I could put my finger on. I knew before venturing to Tuckahoe that the chances of my catching a glimpse of its legendary garden ghost were slim. I must admit, though, to being a little disappointed when I found nothing unusual at all in the photographs I had taken there. I even heard a few days later that a guest of the weekend nuptials claimed to see a woman in "an old wedding gown" near the garden.

My consolation prize for visiting the historic farm was the confirmation by a plantation employee that *something* supernatural was afoot at Tuckahoe. That was reward enough for this paranormal explorer.

⫸ *Whichello* ⫷

*J*ust west of Richmond on River Road stands a building with a reputation for deception, treasure, and of course, ghosts. The site, named "Whichello" after its most infamous owner, was once part of the Randolph's vast Tuckahoe Plantation. Whichello eventually became independent and operated for many decades as a tavern.

Local legend claims that the tavern-keeper, Richard Whichello, was not known for his hospitality or mild temper; rather he was a miserly gambling man with a short fuse and a particularly cruel attitude towards his servants. In 1850, a cattleman is said to have visited the tavern with the profits he'd earned from a recent sale of his herd. The man entertained Richard with a poker game, but lost nearly all of his money in the process. Sometime before the next morning, Richard Whichello was brutally killed with an axe and the cattleman was nowhere to be found.

Though Richard had a nasty reputation, he somehow managed to earn a few friends. Those friends were so concerned that his body, if buried at the local church, would be disinterred and mutilated by local slaves. Their solution was to bury him in secret under the chimney at the east side of the tavern, where his remains still lie today.

Obviously, Richard Whichello's friends could not keep a secret for long and the story of his unusual burial spread – along with rumors that he had been hiding large sums of money on his property for quite some time. Imaginations were kicked into high gear and treasure seekers were soon digging up all parts of the tavern lawn. No treasure was ever found, or rather none reported, thanks to the fear and intimidation carried on by Richard Whichello – from beyond the grave.

Not long after the hunt for his riches began, stories of Whichello appearing on the grounds of his tavern ran rampant. Tenants claimed to hear boots walking the floor late at night and even to hear the voice of the man himself in the dining room.

The threat of some sort of supernatural revenge eventually prompted the treasure-seekers to give up their search. But that didn't stop Whichello from continuing his menacing activity. Workers in the early twentieth century reported seeing a man peering out of a second-story window at them while they painted. There was no one at home at the time.

Whichello Tavern boasts over a century of paranormal activity.

Footsteps, the sounds of doors slamming, and unknown voices in the house were apparently quite common during this period. This activity caught the attention of a previous owner, Mrs. Joseph Crenshaw, who operated a tea shop at Whichello Tavern in the 1930s. She was very interested in the paranormal and allowed séances there on several occasions. One such séance allegedly produced some spirit writing that claimed the tavern-keeper's treasure was buried in the back yard. It was signed "WRW" – the initials of Richard Whichello.

I learned from folks at a nearby restaurant that unexplained activity is still common at the site, but the family who maintains Whichello as a private residence is reluctant to go into detail.

I wondered why the spirit of a man with such a tight pocket would be so eager to tell everyone the whereabouts of his hidden treasure. Does he perhaps have some debt he needs to settle with his conscience before he can move on? Maybe he enjoys watching the living look desperately for something he knows they'll never find. Whatever his reason, Richard Whichello still makes his presence known quite often to travelers on River Road. Most of those travelers report having seen a man in nineteenth-century hunting clothes near the woods at the edge of the lawn – who appears to be searching for something.

If you're paying a visit to Tuckahoe Plantation, remember to slow down and take a careful look at Whichello Tavern – you never know who may be looking back.

❧ Scotchtown ❧

*I*f one follows a handful of signs in Beaverdam, Virginia, they are likely to discover an unusual house with an unusual past. Along with two famous former residents, the home known today as "Scotchtown" boasts a tragic tale of lost love, a killer's burial, and at least one spirit who refuses to move on.

The original plantation house, no longer standing, was thought to have been constructed on the site around 1719 by Charles Chiswell after receiving a land grant from then Lieutenant Governor Alexander Spottswood. Poor records of building during the eighteenth century leave the age of the Scotchtown structure that stands today a mystery, though historians tend to agree that it was likely erected sometime between 1725 and 1750. The house is architecturally unusual for a plantation of the period and has often been referred to as looking more like a barn than a manor.

After Charles Chiswell's death in 1737, ownership of the home transferred to his son, Col. John Chiswell. In order to repay debts owed, John was forced to sell his family estate and move to Williamsburg in 1759. The ownership did not reach far from the family, though, as the buyer was Chiswell's son-in-law, John Robinson. Scotchtown records show no indication that Robinson ever lived in the property; rather it was either vacant or more likely rented to tenant farmers, a common alternative for time.

Col. Chiswell returned to his former home seven years after he left. In 1766, Chiswell murdered a man named Robert Routledge, a merchant from Prince Edward County, in Mosby's Tavern at Cumberland Courthouse, Virginia. Against the wishes of citizens, the members of the court permitted bail for Col. Chiswell. He died while awaiting trial. An issue of the *Gazette* reported that Chiswell's death was caused by "nervous fits owning to a constant uneasiness of the mind." Refused burial in the city of Williamsburg, his body was returned to Scotchtown and interred there. His spirit is thought to be the apparition so often reported roaming the grounds of the estate. Travelers on the nearby rural highway and neighbors of site claim to have witnessed a man in "old fashioned" clothes and a hat at several locations on the property. After watching him for only a few seconds, he simply fades away.

Following the scandal surrounding Chiswell's actions and his death, Scotchtown was sold again in 1770. Records are murky, but it is thought

Scotchtown before its restoration by the APVA. LOC Call Number: HABS VA, 43-BEVDA, 1-8.

that the buyer was John Payne, father of Dolly Madison, who resided there until 1772, when the family moved to their home at Cole's Hill.

After the Paynes left Scotchtown, the property was purchased by a relative of theirs – Patrick Henry. Henry moved in with his family of six children and his wife, Sarah. Not long after their arrival at Scotchtown, Sarah began showing signs of mental illness. As was custom during the eighteenth century, loved ones with "sickness of the brain" were cared for at home. Sarah was confined to a small basement apartment (referred to by some as "dungeon-like") and looked after by a team of servants. Her mental state declined, and it is recorded that she eventually had to be kept in a strait-dress, a restrictive garment similar to a straitjacket.

Henry was heartbroken by his wife's condition and the methods then required for her care. Because of his political importance in the Colony at the time, he was forced to travel often and for long durations. Whenever he was at home, he would spend all of his time with Sarah. Legend has it that he became so emotionally distressed after visiting her that he took to using a small back staircase to return to his room without running into his children. After Sarah's death in 1775, Henry left Scotchtown. He moved to Williamsburg to accept the position as Governor of Virginia, but was plagued for years by the fate of his young wife.

Visitors to Scotchtown today, now operating as a museum, report all manner of paranormal activity. The majority of that activity tends to center around the back stairs and the basement. A guide and a couple on a tour of the first floor of the home were startled by a woman's screams coming from below them – in what was Sarah's room. They ended their tour early.

Many tourists and employees alike have reported a strange "heaviness" in the basement that makes it difficult to breathe. Several have described the sensation as one similar to claustrophobia, even though the basement is roomy and has high ceilings. Could this be some sort of echo of Sarah Henry's emotions during her time at Scotchtown?

If Sarah's spirit still resides in the basement, then Patrick's spirit must certainly be the one walking the back stairs. Volunteers and guides have reported hearing the stair door open and close when no one was in the house. The hollow sound of footsteps has been witnessed on numerous occasions as well. One plantation employee told a chilling story of having to descend the back staircase at night using a flashlight after a power outage. She sensed a strong presence behind her and was frozen with fear for "what felt like forever." The feeling subsided, but she claims that she avoided those stairs at all costs after that night!

Unexplained sounds and uneasy sensations are not the only paranormal phenomena reported at Scotchtown. L.B. Taylor shared a remarkable story in his *Ghosts of Virginia* about a mysterious apparition on the first floor. Several children claimed to see a misty white,

glowing woman in a bedroom. They watched her for a minute or so until she vanished. The children quickly told the adults in another portion of the house what they had witnessed, but the adults were not surprised. Apparently the luminous ghost was quite common.

Scotchtown is cared for today by the Association of the Preservation of Virginia Antiquities. The Association is not only doing a remarkable job of keeping the history of the plantation alive, but they are also keeping the tales of paranormal encounters at the site flowing. Guides and volunteers at Scotchtown are often happy to share their personal experiences of the home's spirits with visitors. Who knows? With a sharp eye or careful ear, you may not need to ask about ghostly encounters there – you may have one of your own.

Scotchtown today.

❧ Kenmore ❧

Fredericksburg has a number of historic haunts, but few can match the provocative tales surrounding Kenmore Plantation. The manor house was built in the 1770s by Fielding Lewis and his wife, Betty Washington Lewis. Betty's brother, George Washington, is thought to have aided in, if not fully executed, the designing the elaborate motifs decorating the ceilings in the home.

Fielding Lewis built the plantation while at his prime. He was a savvy businessman and controlled various shipping ventures, farmed his land for profit, operated a store, and owned a shipyard on the nearby Rappahannock River. His wealth allowed him to establish an armory to assist his fellow patriots in their efforts to overthrow British rule during the Revolutionary War. This generous act drained Lewis' entire fortune and he died, with nothing left but his home, only weeks after the Colonial victory in 1781.

The beautiful Kenmore Plantation in Fredericksburg is an example of early Virginia luxury. LOC Call Number: HABS VA, 89-FRED, 1-29.

Betty remained at the Lewis Farm and successfully managed the property until her death in 1797. The house and grounds changed hands and were eventually purchased by the Gordon family in 1819. They renamed the estate "Kenmore" after their former home in Scotland, and the name has remained unchanged since.

The Gordon family lived at Kenmore until 1859, when they sold the property to Franklin Slaughter. Slaughter is thought to be responsible for the division of the land and the sales of those subdivided tracts, shrinking Kenmore Plantation from over a thousand acres to only a few dozen.

Eventually, the pressures of the encroaching Civil War became too great to endure. Upon Slaughter's evacuation from the estate, the manor house witnessed the effects of war on a deep level. Union troops occupied the home following The Battle of the Wilderness and used the structure as a surgeon's headquarters for the wounded and dying. Many lives were lost at Kenmore during this period, though the exact number remains unknown.

After the war, the plantation became a male academy for several years before returning to service as a private residence. The school days apparently took their toll on the structure because, upon its sale to the Howard family in 1881, the house was reported to be in "deplorable condition." The Howards took painstaking efforts towards the home's restoration and are credited with reviving the Colonial atmosphere that is visible at Kenmore today.

When the Howard family left the plantation in 1914, the estate found itself near the heart of the expanded town of Fredericksburg, no longer on the outskirts as it had once been. Land was at a premium in the Kenmore neighborhood and the bank which owned the manor devised a plan to further subdivide the property and possibly even demolish the eighteenth-century mansion to make way for new construction. A "rescue" committee was quickly formed and funds were raised to purchase the entirety of the Kenmore property. That rescue committee still exists and is now known as The George Washington Foundation. It is solely responsible for the preservation of the historic home and its function as an educational resource for all Americans to enjoy.

Now in the good hands of a caring organization, and long after its century of upheaval and war, one would think that the atmosphere at Kenmore would be calm and quiet. According to several employees, that is not the case. While the home provides a serene glimpse at eighteenth-century life in Virginia, the ghostly occurrences there prompt dozens of questions yet to be answered.

One of the most common things associated with paranormal activity at Kenmore is the sound of heavy footsteps throughout the house. Guides who have been alone in the mansion have reported hearing someone walking on the second floor, on the stairs, and even in the hallway in which they were standing. No one is certain of who

is causing the noises, but they are often attributed to Fielding Lewis as he was said to have a "determined gait."

Fielding Lewis has also been seen in the manor frequently during and since the twentieth century. Tour guides, housekeepers, preservationists, and guests alike have reported entering a room they thought was

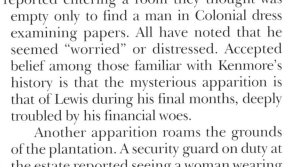

empty only to find a man in Colonial dress examining papers. All have noted that he seemed "worried" or distressed. Accepted belief among those familiar with Kenmore's history is that the mysterious apparition is that of Lewis during his final months, deeply troubled by his financial woes.

Another apparition roams the grounds of the plantation. A security guard on duty at the estate reported seeing a woman wearing a long dress and a veil. She was standing on a walkway near the gate, crossed the path, and vanished. The security guard was no stranger to the unusual happenings at Kenmore, though. He had, on a separate occasion, watched the knob to an unoccupied room slowly turning. Opening the door to inspect the situation, he found no one. Other employees have made similar claims of the doors at Kenmore tending to have minds of their own. Open doors are known to close, and those that are closed often refuse to open, but later move with ease.

With so many distinct paranormal phenomena reported, the question begs to be asked: Are the spirits at Kenmore Plantation there by choice or are they somehow destined for an eternity of unrest? Perhaps the answer is found not with the spirits, but the land itself. Another building on the original Kenmore land has a ghostly reputation that stands on its own – Smythe Cottage.

Phantom footsteps are commonly reported in this ornate drawing room. LOC Call Number: HABS VA, 89-FRED, 1-34.

❧ Smythe Cottage ❧

The appropriately named "Smythe Cottage" was once the home and shop of a blacksmith on the Kenmore estate. The structure that stands at the site now is believed to be a more "modern" building, dating sometime around 1830, constructed on the same location as the blacksmith's shop and built using some of materials from the older cottage. The name, a steady reminder of the site's past, has carried on to present day.

The Cottage has served many purposes over its lifetime, from a private home to a bar and restaurant and now a formal English tea shop named "Pinkadilly Tea." Reports of unexplained events there, however, have remained remarkably unchanged. The family who called Smythe Cottage home during the later portion of the twentieth century recalled several occasions where heavy footsteps were heard by the entire family. The steps, which they noted as "pacing," always sounded as though they were coming from the single room that makes up the second level of the building. No one was ever upstairs when the sounds were heard.

The family's two young sons often told their parents of mysterious apparitions in the house, from phantom lights and mists to humanlike shadows. The boys' mother and father attributed the stories to the active imaginations of children living in an old house – until they saw one for themselves.

The parents suspect that they caught a glimpse of the famous Dark Man of Smythe Cottage. (I love how ghosts are given such romantic names in old towns like Fredericksburg.) Reports of the mysterious figure are always the same: He has long, dark hair pulled back in a low ponytail and wears a knee-length dark coat. He never speaks or makes any gesture offering clues to his identity or his reason for appearing at the site.

More often spotted on the back patio, many claim to have seen the Dark Man inside the Cottage as well. One encounter during the building's service as a bar and restaurant conveys how "real" the apparition seems to those who notice him. A cook working one night in the kitchen at the rear of the building claims to have seen the man standing near the back door. The cook, clearly frightened, went after the Dark Man with a knife. The man simply "faded away," leaving the cook alone, ruffled, and confused. Sightings of the Dark Man have been reported for decades, though it is suspected that he has been witnessed for far longer and those encounters not shared.

The former restaurant owners have reported many stories of poltergeist activity at Smythe Cottage. Silverware has been known to rearrange itself and candles suddenly extinguish for no reason. The current operator of Pinkadilly Tea has even found sugar bowls, empty upon leaving the previous night, all filled when she arrived the next morning.

The Virginia Society of Paranormal Education and Research (VASPER) performed an investigation at the Smythe Cottage in Spring, 2008. While there, investigators witnessed utensils hanging near the kitchen window suddenly begin to rattle and swing. They were unable to recreate the movement by walking, jumping, or bumping the nearby counters and sink. During the same investigation, candle flames were seen burning horizontally even though no drafts were detected.

The VASPER investigation also captured several whispery disembodied voices from inside the structure, though their messages were unclear. Photographs of unusual lights and "auras" from the Smythe Cottage combined with the audio recordings and personal experiences of the investigators during their visit resulted in their declaring the site an "active haunt."

The paranormal activity at Smythe Cottage continues, and folks at Pinkadilly Tea have grown accustomed to it, just as their predecessors had. It seems that mysterious hold of the Kenmore property has reached at least one more spirit and refuses to let go.

Secluded Mountains:
Western Plantations

❧ Red Hill ❦

$\mathcal{A}$sk most Virginians to tell you where Red Hill is located and they'll likely respond only with a puzzled expression. I admit that I stumbled upon it entirely by accident while seeking out sites to include in this book. In searching for information on alleged spirits at a place called Staunton Hill, I contacted a historical society in nearby Lynchburg. I was greeted on the phone by an older lady with a sweet mountain drawl. She was tremendously helpful with names, dates, and people associated with Staunton Hill, but said she was unaware of any ghosts there. "If you're set on ghosts, you should try Red Hill. It's right down the road from Staunton Hill, and I've heard several people tell of a little boy there. Folks say they see him over near the woods for a second or two, and then he's gone." I thanked her and set about planning my trip to Red Hill.

One of our nation's most outspoken patriots, Patrick Henry, retired to a paradise in Brookneal, Virginia, that he named Red Hill. The serene estate is where his remains, and those of close family members, were eventually laid to rest. The farm he built was a collection of simple structures that included a modest frame house, separate law office, carriage house, blacksmith's shop, and servants' quarters. Though the main house was destroyed by fire, generous grants from philanthropist Eugene B. Casey funded the construction of a replica on the original foundation for many generations to learn from and enjoy.

A winding road lined by forest and bordered by a small stream led me to Henry's tranquil hideaway. The landscape was a lush blanket of red, orange, and gold with Virginia's fall foliage in full splendor. I was amazed to discover such a scenic collection of history tucked into the foothills near Lynchburg.

Before beginning my quest for the elusive Boy-Near-the-Woods, I stopped in the museum at the visitor's center to take a look at their impressive collection of Henry family

Patrick Henry's Red Hill (now the Patrick Henry National Memorial) overlooks lush mountaintops in Brookneal, Virginia.

artifacts. I admired a well-preserved violin that had belonged to the statesman himself, and studied a simple writing desk where I imagined he composed dozens of letters to other famous patriots. The showpiece of the exhibit was the painting by Peter Frederick Rothermel of Henry delivering his immortal "Liberty or Death" speech at Richmond's St. John's Church. Though I was already an admirer of this stubborn Founding Father, I noticed a star-struck feeling creep over me when I had taken in the entirety of the museum. I could hardly wait to get out and explore the buildings and the grounds up close.

The structure closest to the visitor's center was the law office. From a distance, it appeared not much larger than a shed. When I stepped closer I found it was a cozy house of two rooms, one outfitted with maps, desks, and other items one would assume necessary in an office of Henry's time. The second room housed two narrow beds and a large fireplace. I read in my tour booklet that the building was seldom used for business, as Henry had officially "retired" upon moving to Red Hill, but used instead as a schoolhouse of sorts where he educated his grown sons in legal affairs. After photographing

The law office.

The interior of Harrison's cabin is welcoming and comfortable.

The graves of Patrick Henry and his second wife, Dorothea Dandridge.

each room and asking a few questions in hopes of capturing a spirit's response in my audio recorder, I headed for a small log house that had caught my eye from the driveway.

A plaque mounted by the door described the log cabin as a recreation of the home of Harrison, a Henry family servant, and his wife and children. I stepped inside and found the first floor quite comfortable. In the center of the room was a large farm table with displays of picked cotton and spun yarn. To my right was another huge fireplace, this one surrounded by iron cooking tools and flanked by an inviting rocking chair. I resisted the urge to make myself at home and collected more photographs for later review.

I stopped next to inspect the herbs in a nearby garden. I was about to move on to the main house when I looked up and noticed a tiny graveyard at the far end of the lawn – just next to the woods.

Camera at the ready, I followed a worn dirt path, peppered with deer tracks, to a family burial plot surrounded by plump boxwoods. The prominent graves were those above ground belonging to Laura Helen Carter, John Henry, Elvira McClelland, and Patrick Henry himself. I had photographed the tombstones of several generations, paid my respects, and was about to leave when I spotted the little obelisk. It was only about two feet tall and was on the opposite side

Little John Henry's grave marker.

of the plot from the other grave markers. A closer look revealed that the stone marked the burial site of John Henry, son of William and Lucy Gray Henry, who died at only one-and-a-half years old. Could he be the Boy-Near-the-Woods? It would make him rather young, but it was worth a try to find out more.

I switched on my audio recorder and placed it near the base of the obelisk. "Hello. My name is Beth. John, if you can hear me, would you mind saying hello near the small box I placed on the ground?" I was waiting eagerly for a reply when the hair on my neck began to rise and my scalp began to tingle. Facing the small grave, my back was to the woods. I managed a quick glance over my shoulder, half expecting to see someone nearby, but found nothing but trees. "Are you here, John?" Another pause. "I have a son who is three years old. How old are you?"

No matter how many times I go through the process of trying to rouse Electronic Voice Phenomena, spirit voices that appear only in recordings, I always seem to spook myself. There's something about the silence between questions and all of the what-ifs that lurk there that makes it hard to suppress one's fight or flight instinct. The more questions I asked there near the woods at Red Hill, the less alone I felt, and that made the struggle with my adrenaline even more difficult. Trying to calm my nerves with my senses at high alert, I continued my questioning.

"Is your family here with you?" A breeze bent the treetops and sent swirls of leaves dancing down around me. The idea that a child *could* still be attached somehow to Red Hill, alone there with no one to comfort him, weighed heavily on my mind. I had tried not to think about it too much before my visit, but standing there by myself in the cold and addressing him directly made the concept too difficult to shake. "Are you happy here, John?"

I paused for a reply when an intense feeling of warmth began to surround me. It started at my ears and spread to the rest of my body in a wave. I felt as comfortable as if I'd been snug in my bed at home. My mind struggled to find a logical cause for the sensation, but eventually surrendered. My sadness for John had been replaced by contentment.

Several minutes later, I thanked whoever may have been near for listening and told them I hoped they were able to respond. After gathering my wits, I walked to the main house for more photographs. The shadows were growing long and dusk was not far off. An ancient Osage Orange tree, proclaimed the oldest in the nation, stood next to the house like a guard. I ventured inside.

The two large rooms and foyer on the first floor were decorated with everyday items of the early nineteenth century which gave an odd illusion that the family had just stepped out for a little while. This illusion did not help to stave off my feeling that I was intruding, like I was some sort of Peeping Tom looking through a window in the present and seeing the past. The sounds of an educational video suddenly echoed from the eastern end of the house and gave me a start. My heart slowed back down when I remembered the attendant in the visitor center telling me that the program ran automatically every fifteen minutes. The booming voices on the video hampered any attempts at my recording an audio track inside, so I decided to have a look at the estate's carriage house and blacksmith's shop before the site closed for the day.

I approached the carriage house from the rear and found it built partway into the hillside. The door at ground level to me was actually an entrance to the loft on the top floor. Inside, there were gourds stored for the winter, bushels of cotton, and dozens of strange looking farm implements. The loft felt cramped with so much stacked against the sloping walls that made up the roofline, and it had the

The rooms in the recreated main house feel as though the family may return at any moment.

An orb appeared in this photo taken in the loft of the carriage house.

same strange atmosphere as the house – like life had just stopped momentarily and that everyone would be right back.

The stairs were blocked off to visitors, but I managed to lean over the rail and take a few pictures anyway. I went back out onto the hill and carefully descended the steep grade to photograph the rest of the building. The shadows had grown much longer and the sun was just barely peaking over the horizon then. I noticed the lavender tone of twilight had already spread to the driveway where I stood, so I quickened my pace.

My final stop at Red Hill was the blacksmith's shop. It was only a short walk down the dirt road from the carriage house. Twilight had surrounded it as well. Tools hung near an enormous stone forge, and attached to the side of the structure was an equally massive bellows, easily five feet in length. The shop, too, had the unusual feeling that work had only momentarily stopped.

Places of work often harbor a surprising amount of paranormal activity. I suppose it makes sense when you consider how much time is spent on the job and how much energy we expend there. "Imprints" of personalities and residual types of scenes seem to be the most common in places of industry. I wondered if that was the case at Red Hill.

I filled my camera with shots of every angle of the blacksmith's shop that I could manage. I noted several lights and blurs when I snapped the images, but never felt any uncomfortable presence.

The quiet of the shop was the perfect setting for another attempt at capturing spirit voices in an audio recording. I

**The blacksmith's shop
proved a peaceful destination.**

switched on the recorder and sat on a bench near the north wall. My questions ranged from "How long have you been a smithy?" to "What keeps you here?" The pauses between questions felt as heavy as those near the cemetery. Darkness was falling, so I said my thanks and trekked uphill to the parking lot to find my car was the only one left.

I drove from Brookneal in a sort of daze, feeling like I'd left too soon. The town itself was straight out of a story book, and Red Hill from the pages of history. Reviewing the data I collected was thrilling

– every image and every second of the audio tracks held the possibility of discovery. I found one photo from the carriage house loft that contained an unexplained light and several from the blacksmith's shop that were dotted with orbs. The audio recordings, however, revealed no messages.

The few anomalies that surfaced in my data from the day were not surprising. The results were average in number and the likelihood of paranormal activity causing the mysterious images was arguable. This certainly does not mean that the estate is lacking its rumored ghost. Remember the old "absence of evidence" saying? I think it applies well here. My visit to Red Hill and the investigative experiments conducted there were only a blink in time, outside of which any amount of paranormal activity could take place.

The feeling that swept over me near the Henry family cemetery and the spine-tingling sensations that accompanied it were more intense than any other I had experienced on my travels to these legendary haunted plantations. Though I'm slightly disappointed that I did not witness the phantom boy with my own eyes, my instincts tell me that *someone* was there.

I doubt they'll be leaving any time soon.

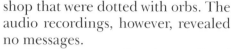

Many photos taken in the shop, like this one, contained orbs and lights.

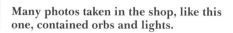

⇛ Belle Grove ⇚

Middletown, Virginia, is a tiny but historic point on the map between Stephens City and Strasburg in the Shenandoah Valley. For such a small place, Middletown boasts several famous haunts, including the Wayside Inn, the Wayside Theatre, Rhodes Tavern, and the Cedar Creek Battlefield. But the stories of jealousy, murder, and restless spirits at Belle Grove Plantation stand high above the rest.

Belle Grove was built by Major Isaac Hite, a William and Mary Alumnus and Revolutionary War veteran, on land given to him by his father, Joist Hite. The massive structure of local limestone was completed in only three years – an impressive feat in 1797. Before moving in to his grand estate, Isaac married Nelly Conway Madison, sister of (then) future President James Madison. Hite's social, financial, and political standings all seemed well secured. His family life, though, took a tragic turn when Nelly died in 1802 and he was left to care for their three children.

Not long after Nelly's death, Isaac remarried. His properties grew to include 7500 acres of land, 103 slaves, a general store, saw mill, grist mill, and a distillery. Hite passed away in 1836, and his second wife, Ann Tunstall Maury, managed the family's holdings until her own death in 1851. Ownership of Belle Grove changed hands several times before it was purchased by Benjamin Cooley in 1860.

Benjamin was a prosperous bachelor and moved into Belle Grove with his servants, including his cook, Harriet. Rumors swirled that Benjamin and Harriet had a relationship that involved more than just food. Harriet was reported to have said on several occasions, "If Master Cooley takes a bride, she won't last long."

Belle Grove sits atop a hill near Middletown.

Those words, however, had a much more sinister meaning than anyone then assumed.

Benjamin did take a bride, a young widow named Hettie. It was common for Harriet and Hettie to exchange harsh words, and sometimes even get into physical altercations. Disrespect towards the lady of the house by any slave was seldom tolerated in mid-nineteenth century Virginia, but Benjamin never stepped in to reprimand his long-time cook. The tension between the two women eventually reached its peak on February 26, 1861.

Hettie had come down to the basement kitchen, possibly to confront the servant about her behavior, when Harriet struck Hettie with some sort of axe or cleaver. She then dragged Mrs. Cooley out to the smokehouse where she apparently intended to destroy the evidence of her crime in the large firepit. Thinking she had finished the job, Harriet fled.

Other farm workers discovered Hettie, bleeding and badly burned, but still alive. They took her into the manor house where she clung to life for three days before finally succumbing to her injuries.

Harriet was soon captured and tried for Hettie Cooley's murder. Witnesses testified that they had seen Harriet near the smokehouse not long before the crime was discovered, and told the judge and jury of the tumultuous relationship between the two women. Harriet was convicted and imprisoned – but not for long. She was sent to the State Penitentiary in Richmond and was freed by the Union Army less than one year after her arrival. Due mostly to the chaos and confusion of war, nothing is known of Harriet's life after her release.

Shortly after his wife's murder in 1861, Benjamin Cooley sold Belle Grove and left the area. Sadly, the estate had not seen the last of the heartache and bloodshed that would come to its grounds. Because it stood near the heart of the conflict, Belle Grove was occupied alternately by both armies during the Civil War for use as a headquarters and hospital at the Battle of Cedar Creek in 1864.

After the war ended, Belle Grove, like the rest of the south, underwent years of repair and restoration. Today, the plantation is preserved by the National Trust for Historic Preservation and is open to the public as a museum. Since its transition from private home to tourist attraction, dozens of visitors and employees of Belle Grove have reported what they believe to be a very restless spirit residing there.

I traveled to Middletown to try and gather more details to the ghostly rumors surrounding the plantation. The townspeople offered an interesting aura to my search with their matter-of-fact belief that Mrs. Cooley was a "regular" at Belle Grove. The employees at the plantation, however, had been instructed to avoid talk of ghosts at all costs and could not answer any of my questions. I didn't give up – I toured the house and grounds and set about collecting my photographs and audio recordings.

While I was stretching my torso over the safety rail to take a shot of the pit in the icehouse, one of the guides approached me with a bit of hesitation. I could tell she was nervous about someone from the main house seeing us talking and I knew right away that she had a ghost story to share.

"I know we're not supposed to talk about it, but I don't think it's something to hide," she said. My eyes widened and I nodded for her to continue. "We're always hearing weird sounds in the house, especially footsteps and voices from the first floor when we're in the

The entrance to the basement is concealed beneath the manor's front portico.

gift shop in the basement." It was just then that it occurred to me the museum office and gift shop were set up where Harriet made her first strike on Hettie with the cleaver. A shiver ran through me. "The floors let a lot of sound through and everything upstairs seems to echo like crazy – but it happens when nobody's there – when we're opening or closing for the day.

"Did you hear about the rugs?" I shook my head and she gave a look back over her shoulder. "Well, a few years ago, we had the rugs sent out for cleaning. The cleaners brought them back when they were done and put them all back in the rooms where they belonged. Only thing was, we weren't here at the time. They came too early."

"How did they get in?" I asked.

"When we called to ask them that same question, they said a woman in a costume met them at the door and pointed them where they needed to go. The burglar alarm was never set off. We still have no idea what went on that morning. Lots of people say they've seen that woman looking out of one of the upstairs windows.

"Someone also told me that a UPS driver met a ghost face-to-face before I came to work here. He said the driver was making a delivery to the gift shop one morning and a little girl opened the door for him. He scared the dickens out of the manager – she hadn't even unlocked the door for the day yet. He told her that her daughter had let him in, but she said she didn't have a daughter and there was no one there besides her. The man went white as a sheet!"

A ghostly woman is rumored to be seen in the windows of Belle Grove.

The woman adjusted her jacket and turned again to look back over her shoulder towards the main house. "I've got to hurry, but make sure you get back to the old slave cemetery before you leave – that's another spot where a lot of weird things happen. Every once in a while we get someone asking where the singing back there is coming from."

After expressing my thanks, the guide wished me luck and hurried off towards the parking lot. My mind was flooded with images of the gruesome murder story and the accounts the woman had just shared. The combination of the two sent that peculiar tingle over my scalp as I stood alone near the doorway of the dark icehouse. With my senses on high alert, I headed toward the slave cemetery.

The little road that led between the manor house and the enormous twentieth-century barn happened to also pass by the site where the smokehouse Harriet had used to "dispose" of Mrs. Cooley once stood. All that was left of the building were a few foundation stones and a fire pit. I photographed the area and continued down the path.

A beautifully recreated apple orchard lay at the end of the road, and just beside it was the largest slave cemetery I'd ever

The sounds of singing have been heard coming from the plantation's slave cemetery.

seen. My house could have easily fit inside the graveyard fence with plenty of room to spare. A huge tree, stripped of its leaves, sat at the far corner and cast gnarled shadows on several of the rough granite grave markers. None bore any inscription. Maybe it was the nameless stones dotting the ground stirring something in the back of my mind, or perhaps it was the barren landscape and strange light that made me feel ill at ease. I had lots of questions, but knew without a doubt the sadness that hung over that portion of the estate was thick.

Of course, spurred by the guide's mention of singing, I couldn't leave before making an audio recording. I pulled my recorder out of my bag, placed it on the ground under the naked tree, and sat near the fence a few feet away from it. I asked several questions about life at the plantation, the names of anyone listening, and finally requested a work song or hymn. The annoying scalp-tingle came back, only much more intense. I waited a few minutes for it to subside and wrapped up the audio session to head home.

My visit to Belle Grove was fascinating, both for the plantation's history and its mystery. My photographs and audio recording from the day offered no clues to the identities of any of the elusive spirits at the estate, but Hettie Cooley certainly has the strongest reason to linger. Even without a first-hand encounter of my own, the urgency and secrecy about the unexplained happenings in the house gave me a firm belief of spirits' existence there. I feel certain that the paranormal activity in Middletown will continue, and until Hettie finds peace, Belle Grove will remain one of the most haunted sites there.

⫸ *Visitor's Guide* ⫷

Adam Thoroughgood House

Address: 1636 Parish Road
Virginia Beach, VA 23455
Phone: (804) 460-7588
Web: www.vbgov.com

Appomattox Manor

c/o: Petersburg National Battlefield
Address: 5001 Siege Road, Petersburg, VA 23803
Phone: (804) 732-3531 ext. 200
Web: www.nps.gov/pete/planyourvisit/directions.htm

Bacon's Castle

c/o: APVA Preservation Virginia
Address: 465 Bacon's Castle Trail
Surry, VA 23883
Phone: (757) 357-5976
Web: www.apva.org/baconscastle

Belle Grove Plantation

Address: 336 Belle Grove Road
Middletown, VA 22645
Phone: (540) 869-2028
Web: www.bellegrove.org

Berkeley Plantation

Address: 12602 Harrison Landing Road
Charles City, VA 23030
Phone: (804) 829-6018
Web: www.berkeleyplantation.com

Endview Plantation

Address: 362 Yorktown Road
Newport News, VA 23603
Phone: (757) 887-1862
Web: www.endview.org

Eppington Plantation

c/o: Eppington Foundation
Address: 14201 Eppes Falls Road
Chesterfield, VA 23838
Phone: (804) 748-1624
Web: www.co.chesterfield.va.us/tourism/eppington.asp

Kenmore Plantation

c/o: The George Washington Foundation
Address: 1201 Washington Avenue
Fredericksburg, VA 22401
Phone: (540) 373-3381
Web: www.kenmore.org

Kittiewan Plantation

c/o: Archeological Society of Virginia
Address: 12104 Weyanoke Road
Charles City, VA 23030
Phone: (804) 829-2272
Web: www.kittiewanplantation.org

Piney Grove at Southall's Plantation

Address: 16920 Southall Plantation Lane
Charles City, VA 23030
Phone: (804) 829-2480
Web: www.pineygrove.com

Prestwould Plantation

Address: 429 Prestwould Drive
Clarksville, VA 23927
Phone: (434) 374-8672
Web: www.scalamandre.com/tour/prest/prest.htm

Red Hill

c/o: Patrick Henry National Memorial
Address: 1250 Red Hill Road
Brookneal, VA 24528
Phone: (434) 376-2044
Web: www.redhill.org

Rosewell

c/o: The Rosewell Foundation
Address: PO BOX 1456
Gloucester, VA 23061
Phone: (804) 693-2585
Web: www.rosewell.org

Scotchtown

c/o: APVA
Address: 16120 Chiswell Lane
Beaverdam, VA 23015
Phone: (804) 227-3500
Web: www.apva.org/scotchtown

Shirley Plantation

Address: 501 Shirley Plantation Road
Charles City, VA 23030
Phone: (804) 829-5121
Web: www.shirleyplantation.com